P9-CAA-571

Betty Crocker's

RED SPOON COLLECTION™

BEST RECIPES FOR

CHICKEN

PRENTICE HALL PRESS

New York   London   Toronto   Sydney   Tokyo

Copyright © 1989 by General Mills, Inc.,
Minneapolis, Minnesota
All rights reserved, including the right of
reproduction in whole or in part in any form.

Published by Prentice Hall Press
A Division of Simon & Schuster, Inc.
Gulf+Western Building
One Gulf+Western Plaza
New York, NY 10023

Published simultaneously in Canada by
Prentice Hall Canada Inc.

PRENTICE HALL PRESS is a registered
trademark of Simon & Schuster, Inc.

BETTY CROCKER is a registered trademark of
General Mills, Inc.

RED SPOON COLLECTION is a trademark of
General Mills, Inc.

Library of Congress Cataloging-in-Publication

Betty Crocker's Red Spoon collection. Chicken.
      p.   cm.
   Includes index.
   ISBN 0-13-073065-3 : $9.95
   1. Cookery (Chicken)
   TX750.5.C45B47 1989
   641.6′65—dc19   88-26585
                          CIP

Manufactured in the United States of America

10 9 8 7 6 5 4 3 2 1

First Prentice Hall Press Edition

CONTENTS

INTRODUCTION

Chicken

Roast chicken for Sunday dinner has long been a fixture of American life, but chicken has come a long way. Chickens are plumper and more dependable than ever, and with this book in hand you won't find yourself at a loss for delicious and varied chicken recipes. Chicken is perhaps the most versatile and economical meat you can buy. It provides you with complete protein and is naturally lean. If reducing your calorie intake, feature chicken in your diet and then reduce calories further by removing the skin. You can even skim fat from soups and stews made with chicken (especially easy if they are chilled first).

Choose Your Chicken

Which chicken is right for the sort of dish you have in mind? Consider how many people you are planning to serve and whether you want leftovers, then choose from the following:

- Broiler-Fryer: These chickens, weighing anywhere from 2½ to 3½ pounds, are all-purpose birds. Broiler-fryers can be found in most markets.

- Roaster: Somewhat older than broiler-fryers, roasters weigh in anywhere from 3½ to 6 pounds. Look for a plump roaster.
- Capon: These birds weigh from 4 to 7 pounds and roast beautifully. They have a high ratio of light to dark meat. A capon is a desexed male bird.
- Stewing Chicken (hen): These birds are older—less tender—and therefore good for stewing or long simmering. They weight 4½ to 6 pounds. True stewing chickens are becoming somewhat hard to find; a roaster is the more expensive substitute.
- Rock Cornish Hen (game hen): These birds are bred for their small size and weigh 1 to 1½ pounds. Half of one game hen is the usual portion. Make the most of these hens by roasting or broiling them.

How to Buy Chicken

When you buy chicken, plan on about ¾ pound per person; this includes the weight of the bones. You can buy chicken whole or cut into parts. If you are not planning to cook a whole bird, buying parts is convenient, but it can cost you more. Buying chicken parts is also convenient because you can choose exactly those portions you like the best, with dark or light meat. Parts vary in cost; wings have the least meat per pound (and are usually the least expensive), and breasts without ribs have the most.

You can save money by buying whole chicken breasts and boning them yourself. With a little practice, you'll be able to do it quickly; we show you how on page 102. Similarly, if you know how to cut a chicken into parts, you are a step ahead in the cost game, too; directions for cutting up a chicken are on pages 100–101.

A word of caution: Don't stock up on chicken unless you intend to freeze it for later use; fresh or thawed chicken will keep in the refrigerator no longer than two days. For tips on storing, freezing and thawing chicken and chicken dishes, turn to the Red Spoon Tips section, pages 97 and 98.

At the Table

How do people learn to carve poultry? It used to be that boys learned from their fathers, but somehow carving seems to be a dying art. There is no reason why everyone can't be a whiz at carving, and it is a simple matter to learn your way around a bird. Find a sturdy, long-tined fork and a sharp carving knife, and turn to page 104 for a quick lesson.

Of course, this book offers you the tastiest Sunday roast chicken. You will also find an inspiring collection of international favorites: Chicken Cacciatore, Chicken and Rice with Curry Sauce, Chicken with Golden Pilaf and Paella. We bring you wonderful recipes for entertaining—Chicken and Artichoke Fondue and Coq au Vin—and such cosy, warming dishes as Brunswick-style Stew and classic Chicken Fricassee with Chive Dumplings. We think you'll agree: Chicken never had it so good.

THE BETTY CROCKER EDITORS

· 1 ·

CHICKEN BASICS

Poached Chicken

3 TO 4 CUPS CUT-UP COOKED CHICKEN

2 ½- to 3-pound broiler-fryer chicken,
  cut up
¼ cup water
½ teaspoon salt

Remove any excess fat from chicken. Place chicken and water in Dutch oven; sprinkle with salt. Heat to boiling; reduce heat. Cover and simmer until thickest pieces are done, 45 to 60 minutes. Remove chicken from bones and skin. Cover and refrigerate up to 2 days.

Cooked Giblets

Giblets (gizzard, heart, liver) and neck
1 ½ cups water
½ teaspoon salt
1 small onion, cut into fourths

Heat all ingredients to boiling in saucepan. Cover and simmer until liver is no longer pink, 5 to 10 minutes. Remove liver; cover and refrigerate. Cover and simmer remaining giblets until gizzard is fork-tender, 30 to 90 minutes.

Refrigerate giblets and broth separately until ready to use. Giblet broth can be used in stuffing, gravy and recipes where chicken broth is specified. Cooked giblets can be cut up and added to gravy and stuffing or used in recipes calling for cut-up cooked chicken.

Simmered Chicken and Chicken Broth

3- to 3½-pound broiler-fryer chicken,
* cut up**
4½ cups water
½ cup chopped celery (with leaves)
1 medium carrot, sliced (about ½ cup)
1½ teaspoons salt
½ teaspoon pepper
1 small onion, sliced
1 sprig parsley

Remove any excess fat from chicken. Place chicken, giblets and neck in Dutch oven. Add remaining ingredients. Heat to boiling; reduce heat. Cover and simmer until thickest pieces of chicken are done, about 45 minutes.

Remove chicken from broth; cool chicken just until cool enough to handle, about 10 minutes. (If desired, refrigerate chicken in broth until cool.) Remove chicken from bones and skin in pieces as large as possible. If not using chicken immediately, cover and refrigerate; use within 24 hours.

Skim fat from broth. Cover and refrigerate if using within 24 hours or freeze for future use.

*3- to 3½ pounds chicken necks, backs and giblets can be used to make broth.

Note: To cook a 4- to 6-pound stewing chicken, increase water to 7 cups and salt to 1 tablespoon. Increase simmering time to about 2½ hours. Yields about 5 cups cut-up cooked chicken and 5 to 6 cups broth.

Roast Chicken

2 1/2- to 3-pound broiler-fryer chicken*
Salt, if desired
Herbed Bread Stuffing (below)
1/4 cup margarine or butter, melted

Rub cavity of chicken lightly with salt, if desired. Do not salt cavity if chicken is to be stuffed. Stuff chicken just before roasting—not ahead of time. Fill wishbone area with stuffing first. Fasten neck skin to back with skewer. Fold wings across back with tips touching. Fill body cavity lightly. (Do not pack—stuffing will expand while cooking.) Tie or skewer drumsticks to tail. Place chicken, breast up, on rack in shallow roasting pan. Brush with margarine. Do not add water or cover pan.

Cook uncovered in 375° oven, until thickest parts of chicken are done and drumstick meat feels very soft when pressed between protected fingers, 1 1/2 to 1 3/4 hours.

Herbed Bread Stuffing

1/2 cup chopped celery (with leaves)
1/4 cup finely chopped onion
1/3 cup margarine or butter
3 cups soft bread cubes
1/2 teaspoon dried sage leaves
1/4 teaspoon salt
1/4 teaspoon dried thyme leaves
1/8 teaspoon pepper

Cook and stir celery and onion in margarine in 10-inch skillet until onion is tender. Stir in about 1 cup of the bread cubes. Turn into deep bowl. Add remaining ingredients; toss. Stuff chicken just before roasting.

Note: To cook stuffing separately, turn into ungreased 1-quart casserole. Cover and cook in 400° oven 30 minutes, 375° oven 40 minutes.

CORN BREAD STUFFING: Substitute corn bread cubes for the soft bread cubes.

GIBLET STUFFING: Chop Cooked Giblets (page 7) and add with the remaining ingredients.

Following pages: Roast Chicken

Microwave Stuffed Chicken

Herbed Bread Stuffing (page 9)
3 1/2-pound broiler-fryer chicken
1/4 cup margarine or butter, melted
1/2 teaspoon paprika

Prepare Herbed Bread Stuffing. Prepare and stuff chicken, except use wooden skewer. Mix margarine and paprika; brush half of the mixture over chicken. Place chicken, breast down, on microwave rack in microwavable dish. Cover with waxed paper and microwave on medium-high (70%) 15 minutes. Turn chicken, breast up. Brush with remaining margarine mixture. Cover and microwave until drumstick meat feels soft when pressed between fingers, 13 to 18 minutes longer. Let stand covered 15 minutes. Release drumsticks from tail.

Chicken Gravy

For each cup gravy:

2 tablespoons drippings (fat and juices)
2 tablespoons all-purpose flour
1 cup Chicken Broth* (page 8)
Salt and pepper, to taste

Place chicken on warm platter; keep warm while preparing gravy. Pour drippings from roasting pan or skillet into bowl, leaving brown particles in pan. Return 2 tablespoons drippings to pan. (Measure accurately because too little fat will make gravy lumpy.)

Stir in flour. (Measure accurately so gravy will not be greasy.) Cook over low heat, stirring constantly, until mixture is smooth and bubbly. Remove from heat; stir in broth. Heat to boiling, stirring constantly. Boil and stir 1 minute. Stir in few drops bottled browning sauce, if desired. If thinner gravy is desired, stir in additional broth or other liquid. Sprinkle with salt and pepper.

*Vegetable cooking water, tomato or vegetable juice can be substituted for part of the broth.

STOVETOP CLASSICS

Batter-fried Chicken

6 OR 7 SERVINGS

2 1/2- to 3-pound broiler-fryer chicken,
   cut up
1/4 cup water
1/3 cup all-purpose flour
1/2 teaspoon salt
1/2 teaspoon celery salt
1/4 teaspoon pepper
Vegetable oil
Thin Fritter Batter (below)

Heat chicken and water to boiling in Dutch oven; reduce heat. Cover and simmer 25 minutes. Remove chicken from Dutch oven; pat dry. Mix flour, salt, celery salt and pepper; coat chicken.

Heat oil (2 to 3 inches) in deep-fat fryer or kettle to 360°. Prepare Thin Fritter Batter. Dip chicken pieces, one at a time, into batter. Fry chicken in oil, 3 or 4 pieces at a time, until golden brown, 5 to 7 minutes.

THIN FRITTER BATTER

1 cup all-purpose flour
1 cup milk
1/4 cup vegetable oil
1 teaspoon baking powder
1/2 teaspoon salt
1 egg

Beat all ingredients with hand beater until smooth.

Fried Chicken

6 OR 7 SERVINGS

1/3 cup all-purpose flour
1 teaspoon salt
1/2 teaspoon paprika
1/4 teaspoon pepper
2 1/2- to 3-pound broiler-fryer chicken,
  cut up
Vegetable oil

Mix flour, salt, paprika and pepper; coat chicken. Heat oil (1/4 inch) in 12-inch skillet until hot. Cook chicken in oil over medium heat until brown, about 15 minutes; reduce heat. Cover tightly and simmer, turning once or twice, until thickest pieces are done, 30 to 40 minutes. If skillet cannot be covered tightly, add 1 to 2 tablespoons water. Remove cover during last 5 minutes of cooking to crisp chicken. Prepare Chicken Gravy (page 12), if desired.

MARYLAND FRIED CHICKEN: Mix 2 eggs and 2 tablespoons water; after coating chicken, dip into egg mixture, then into 2 cups cracker crumbs or dry bread crumbs.

Golden Chicken Nuggets

4 SERVINGS

Vegetable oil
1/3 cup all-purpose flour
1/4 teaspoon salt
1 1/2 teaspoons vinegar
1/4 teaspoon baking soda
1/3 cup water
1 large whole chicken breast (about 1
  pound), boned, skinned and cut into
  1 × 1/2-inch pieces
Sweet-and-Sour Sauce (below) or soy
  sauce

Heat oil (2 to 3 inches) in deep-fat fryer or saucepan to 360°. Mix flour and salt. Mix vinegar and baking soda. Stir vinegar mixture and water into flour mixture; beat until smooth. Dip chicken into batter; allow excess batter to drip into bowl. Fry chicken, 4 or 5 pieces at a time, turning once, until golden brown, about 4 minutes; drain. Serve with Sweet-and-Sour Sauce.

SWEET-AND-SOUR SAUCE

1/4 cup chili sauce
1/4 cup plum or grape jelly

Heat chili sauce and plum jelly over low heat, stirring constantly, until jelly is melted.

Stir-fried Chicken and Vegetables

2 large whole chicken breasts (about 2 pounds), boned and skinned*
1 teaspoon salt
1 teaspoon cornstarch
1 teaspoon soy sauce
1 egg white
6 ounces Chinese pea pods, or 1 package (6 ounces) frozen Chinese pea pods, partially thawed
2 tablespoons vegetable oil
1 teaspoon finely chopped gingerroot or 1/2 teaspoon ground ginger
2 cloves garlic, finely chopped
6 medium stalks celery, cut diagonally into 1/4-inch slices (about 3 cups)
4 ounces mushrooms, sliced (about 2 cups)
1 can (8 ounces) water chestnuts, drained and sliced
1 can (8 ounces) sliced bamboo shoots, drained
2 tablespoons vegetable oil
3/4 cup water
1 teaspoon instant chicken bouillon
1/2 teaspoon sugar
1/4 cup cold water
2 tablespoons cornstarch
1 teaspoon soy sauce

Cut chicken into strips, 1½ × ¼ inch. Toss chicken, salt, 1 teaspoon cornstarch, 1 teaspoon soy sauce and the egg white in glass or plastic bowl. Cover and refrigerate 30 minutes.

Remove strings from pea pods. Heat 2 tablespoons oil in wok or 12-inch skillet over medium heat until hot. Cook and stir gingerroot and garlic in oil until light brown. Add pea pods and celery; stir-fry 1 minute. Add mushrooms, water chestnuts and bamboo shoots; stir-fry 1 minute. Remove vegetables with slotted spoon.

Heat 2 tablespoons oil in wok over high heat until hot. Add chicken; stir-fry until chicken is white, about 2 minutes. Stir in ¾ cup water, the bouillon (dry) and sugar. Heat to boiling; reduce heat. Cover and simmer, stirring occasionally, 2 minutes longer.

Mix ¼ cup water and 2 tablespoons cornstarch; stir into chicken mixture. Heat to boiling, stirring constantly. Boil and stir 1 minute. Add vegetables and 1 teaspoon soy sauce. Cook and stir until hot, 1 to 2 minutes. Serve with additional soy sauce, if desired.

*Freeze chicken about 1½ hours before preparing recipe—it will be much easier to cut into slices.

Following pages: Maryland Fried Chicken

Coq au Vin

1/3 cup all-purpose flour
1 teaspoon salt
1/4 teaspoon pepper
2 1/2- to 3-pound broiler-fryer chicken,
    cut up
8 slices bacon
8 small onions
8 ounces mushrooms, sliced (about 3
    cups)
4 medium carrots, cut into halves
1 cup Chicken Broth (page 8)
1 cup dry red wine
1/2 teaspoon salt
1 clove garlic, crushed
Bouquet garni*

Mix flour, 1 teaspoon salt and the pepper; coat chicken. Fry bacon in 12-inch skillet until crisp; drain. Cook chicken in bacon fat until brown, about 15 minutes.

Push chicken to side; add onions and mushrooms. Cook and stir until mushrooms are tender. Drain fat from skillet. Crumble bacon and stir into vegetables with the remaining ingredients. Cover and simmer until thickest pieces of chicken are done, about 35 minutes. Remove bouquet garni; skim off excess fat. Sprinkle chicken with snipped parsley, if desired.

*Tie 1/2 teaspoon dried thyme leaves, 2 large sprigs parsley and 1 bay leaf in cheesecloth bag or place in tea ball.

Chicken Provençal

2 1/2- to 3-pound broiler-fryer chicken
1/3 cup all-purpose flour
1 teaspoon paprika
1 teaspoon dried basil leaves
1/2 teaspoon salt
1/2 teaspoon dried oregano leaves
1/4 teaspoon pepper
1/4 teaspoon dried marjoram leaves
3 tablespoons vegetable oil
16 small pitted ripe olives
8 medium carrots, cut into fourths
8 small whole onions
4 medium potatoes, cut into fourths
1 cup Chicken Broth (page 8)
1 tablespoon cornstarch
1 tablespoon cold water

Cut chicken into pieces; cut each breast half into halves and remove skin. Mix flour, paprika, basil, salt, oregano, pepper and marjoram. Coat chicken with flour mixture. Heat oil in 4-quart Dutch oven until hot. Cook chicken until brown on all sides, about 15 minutes. Add olives, carrots, onions and potatoes; pour broth over vegetables. Heat to boiling; reduce heat. Cover and cook until chicken is done, about 45 minutes. Remove chicken and vegetables; keep warm. Mix cornstarch and cold water; stir into liquid in Dutch oven. Heat to boiling, stirring constantly. Boil and stir 1 minute. Serve sauce with chicken.

Braised Chicken with Vegetables

6 OR 7 SERVINGS

1/3 cup all-purpose flour

1 teaspoon salt

1/2 teaspoon paprika

1/8 teaspoon pepper

2 1/2- to 3-pound broiler-fryer chicken, cut up

2 tablespoons vegetable oil

1/4 cup water

2 medium carrots, cut into 1/4-inch slices

8 ounces broccoli, cut into flowerets (about 2 cups)*

1/2 small head cauliflower, cut into flowerets (about 2 cups)

1/2 teaspoon onion salt

1/2 teaspoon dried rosemary leaves, crushed, dried thyme leaves or dried dill weed

1/2 cup dairy sour cream

Mix flour, salt, paprika and pepper; coat chicken. Heat oil in 12-inch skillet or Dutch oven until hot. Cook chicken in oil over medium heat until brown, about 15 minutes. Drain fat from skillet if necessary.

Add water and carrots to skillet. Heat to boiling; reduce heat. Cover and simmer 30 minutes. Add broccoli and cauliflower; sprinkle with onion salt and rosemary. Add small amount water if necessary. Cover and simmer until thickest pieces of chicken are done and broccoli is crisp-tender, 10 to 20 minutes.

Remove chicken and vegetables to warm platter with slotted spoon; keep warm. Stir sour cream into skillet; heat just until hot. Serve with chicken and vegetables.

*8 ounces fresh green beans, cut into 1-inch pieces (about 1 1/2 cups), 2 small zucchini, sliced, or 1 1/2 cups frozen green peas, thawed, can be substituted for the broccoli. If using green beans, add with the carrots.

Chicken Cacciatore

1/3 cup all-purpose flour
1 teaspoon salt
1/4 teaspoon pepper
2 1/2- to 3-pound broiler-fryer chicken,
    cut up
1/4 cup olive or vegetable oil
1 cup sliced mushrooms (about 3 ounces)
1 medium onion, chopped (about 1/2 cup)
1/4 cup water
1/4 cup sliced ripe olives
1 teaspoon salt
1 teaspoon crushed dried oregano leaves
1/4 teaspoon pepper
1 can (16 ounces) whole tomatoes,
    undrained
1 can (8 ounces) tomato sauce
2 cloves garlic, crushed
1 bay leaf
Snipped parsley
Hot cooked spaghetti

Mix flour, 1 teaspoon salt and 1/4 teaspoon pepper; coat chicken. Heat oil in 12-inch skillet or Dutch oven until hot. Cook chicken in oil over medium heat until brown, about 15 minutes. Drain fat from skillet.

Mix remaining ingredients except parsley and spaghetti; break up tomatoes with fork. Pour over chicken. Heat to boiling; reduce heat. Cover and simmer until thickest pieces of chicken are done, 30 to 40 minutes. Sprinkle with parsley; serve with spaghetti.

Chicken Ratatouille

⅓ cup all-purpose flour
1 teaspoon salt
1 teaspoon paprika
⅛ teaspoon pepper
2½- to 3-pound broiler-fryer chicken,
  cut up
3 tablespoons vegetable oil
¼ cup water
1½ teaspoons garlic salt
1 teaspoon dried basil leaves
¼ teaspoon pepper
1 small eggplant (about 1 pound), cut
  into 1-inch pieces (4 to 5 cups)
2 small zucchini (about ½ pound), sliced
1 medium green pepper, cut into 1-inch
  pieces
1 medium onion, chopped
3 medium tomatoes, cut into wedges
¼ teaspoon salt
Grated Parmesan cheese

Mix flour, 1 teaspoon salt, the paprika and ⅛ teaspoon pepper; coat chicken. Heat oil in 12-inch skillet or Dutch oven until hot. Cook chicken in oil over medium heat until brown, about 15 minutes. Drain fat from skillet; add water. Heat to boiling; reduce heat. Cover and simmer 20 minutes.

Mix garlic salt, basil and ¼ teaspoon pepper. Add eggplant to skillet; sprinkle with half of the garlic salt mixture. Add zucchini, green pepper and onion; sprinkle with remaining garlic salt mixture. Add 1 to 2 tablespoons water if necessary. Cover and simmer, stirring occasionally, until thickest pieces of chicken are done and vegetables are crisp-tender, 10 to 15 minutes. Add tomato wedges; sprinkle with ¼ teaspoon salt. Cover and simmer until tomatoes are hot, about 5 minutes. Serve with cheese and, if desired, hot cooked rice.

Following pages: Chicken Ratatouille

Chicken à la King

1 can (4 ounces) mushroom stems and
  pieces, drained (reserve liquid)
1 small green pepper, chopped (about ½
  cup)
½ cup margarine or butter
½ cup all-purpose flour
1 teaspoon salt
¼ teaspoon pepper
1½ cups milk
1¼ cups water
1½ teaspoons instant chicken bouillon
2 cups cut-up cooked chicken
1 jar (2 ounces) chopped pimientos,
  drained
Corn bread*

Cook and stir mushrooms and green pepper in margarine over medium heat 5 minutes. Stir in flour, salt and pepper. Cook over low heat, stirring constantly, until bubbly. Remove from heat; stir in milk, water, reserved mushroom liquid and bouillon (dry). Heat to boiling, stirring constantly. Boil and stir 1 minute. Stir in chicken and pimientos; heat until hot. Serve over corn bread.

*Toast, waffles, hot mashed potatoes, hot cooked rice or noodles, patty shells or baking powder biscuits can be substituted for the corn bread.

Chicken Piccata

3 chicken breast halves (about 1½
  pounds)
1 egg, slightly beaten
1 tablespoon water
½ cup dry bread crumbs
½ teaspoon salt
¼ teaspoon pepper
⅛ teaspoon garlic powder
¼ cup all-purpose flour
2 tablespoons margarine or butter
2 tablespoons vegetable oil
2 tablespoons lemon juice
2 tablespoons dry white wine

Skin, bone and cut each chicken breast half into halves. Mix egg and water. Mix bread crumbs, salt, pepper and garlic powder. Coat chicken with flour; dip into egg mixture. Coat with crumb mixture. Heat 1 tablespoon margarine and 1 tablespoon oil in 10-inch skillet over medium heat until hot. Cook 3 pieces chicken, turning once, until done, about 8 minutes. Remove chicken from skillet; keep warm. Repeat with remaining margarine, oil and chicken. Remove chicken from skillet; stir lemon juice and wine into skillet. Heat to boiling; pour over chicken. Sprinkle with snipped parsley and serve with lemon wedges, if desired.

French Chicken Fricassee

2 medium carrots, sliced (about 1 cup)
1 medium onion, sliced
1 medium stalk celery, sliced (about ¹/₂ cup)
¹/₄ cup margarine or butter
2¹/₂- to 3-pound broiler-fryer chicken, cut up
2 cups water
1 cup dry white wine
2 teaspoons instant chicken bouillon
¹/₂ teaspoon salt
2 bouquets garnis*
16 small white onions
2 tablespoons margarine or butter
1 tablespoon lemon juice
8 ounces mushrooms, sliced (about 3 cups)
¹/₂ cup whipping cream
2 egg yolks
2 tablespoons snipped parsley
4 to 5 cups hot cooked noodles

Cook and stir carrots, sliced onion and celery in ¹/₄ cup margarine in 12-inch skillet or Dutch oven over medium heat until onion is tender; push to side. Add chicken; cook until light brown, about 10 minutes. Add water, ¹/₂ cup of the wine, the bouillon (dry), salt and 1 bouquet garni. Heat to boiling; reduce heat. Cover and simmer until thickest pieces of chicken are done, about 40 minutes.

Heat 16 onions, 2 tablespoons margarine, remaining wine and bouquet garni to boiling; reduce heat. Cover and simmer until onions are tender, about 25 minutes. Remove chicken and whole onions to warm platter with slotted spoon. Strain bouillon and onion liquids together; discard carrot, onion and celery slices. Skim fat from broth. Heat broth, lemon juice and mushrooms to boiling; reduce heat. Simmer uncovered until reduced to 2¹/₂ cups.

Mix whipping cream and egg yolks. Beat 1 cup of the broth by tablespoonfuls into whipping cream mixture. Beat in remaining broth. Heat to boiling, stirring constantly. Boil and stir 1 minute; pour over chicken and onions. Sprinkle with parsley; serve with noodles.

*For each bouquet garni, tie ¹/₈ teaspoon dried rosemary leaves, 2 sprigs parsley and ¹/₂ bay leaf in cheesecloth bag or place in tea ball.

Chicken Fricassee with Chive Dumplings

6 OR 7 SERVINGS

⅓ cup all-purpose flour
1 teaspoon salt
1 teaspoon paprika
¼ teaspoon pepper
3- to 3½-pound broiler-fryer chicken,
    cut up
Vegetable oil
1 cup water
3 tablespoons all-purpose flour
Milk
Chive Dumplings (below)

Mix ⅓ cup flour, the salt, paprika and pepper; coat chicken. Heat thin layer of oil in 12-inch skillet until hot. Cook chicken in oil over medium heat until brown, about 15 minutes. Drain fat from skillet; reserve. Add water and, if desired, chopped onion, lemon juice or herbs, such as dried rosemary or thyme leaves, to chicken. Heat to boiling; reduce heat. Cover and simmer until thickest pieces of chicken are done, 30 to 40 minutes. Remove chicken to warm platter; keep warm. Drain liquid from skillet; reserve.

Heat 3 tablespoons of the reserved fat in skillet. Blend in 3 tablespoons flour. Cook over low heat, stirring constantly, until mixture is smooth and bubbly; remove from heat. Add enough milk to reserved liquid to measure 3 cups; pour into skillet. Heat to boiling, stirring constantly. Boil and stir 1 minute. Add chicken.

Prepare Chive Dumplings; drop by spoonfuls onto hot chicken. Cook uncovered 10 minutes; cover and cook 20 minutes longer.

CHIVE DUMPLINGS

1½ cups all-purpose flour
3 tablespoons snipped chives
2 teaspoons baking powder
¾ teaspoon salt
3 tablespoons shortening
¾ cup milk

Mix flour, chives, baking powder and salt; cut in shortening until mixture resembles fine crumbs. Stir in milk.

Chicken Almond

1 large whole chicken breast (about 1
  pound), boned and skinned*
2 tablespoons vegetable oil
1/2 teaspoon salt
8 ounces mushrooms, cut into 1/4-inch
  slices (about 3 cups)
1 cup sliced peeled bamboo shoots or 1
  can (8 ounces) sliced bamboo shoots,
  drained
1 large stalk celery, cut diagonally into
  1/4-inch slices (about 3/4 cup)
1/4 teaspoon ground ginger
3/4 cup Chicken Broth (page 8)
2 teaspoons soy sauce
3 tablespoons cold water
2 tablespoons cornstarch
1/2 cup toasted whole blanched almonds
2 to 3 cups hot cooked rice

Cut chicken into 1/8-inch slices. Heat oil and
salt in 10-inch skillet over medium-high heat
until few drops water sprinkled in skillet skitter
around. Add chicken. Cook, stirring frequently,
until almost done, about 6 minutes.

Add mushrooms, bamboo shoots, celery and
ginger. Cook and stir 1 minute. Stir in broth
and soy sauce; reduce heat. Cover and simmer
until chicken is done and vegetables are crisp-
tender, 3 to 5 minutes.

Shake cold water and cornstarch in tightly covered container; gradually stir into chicken mixture. Heat to boiling, stirring constantly. Boil
and stir 1 minute. Top with almonds and serve
with rice.

*Freeze chicken about 1 1/2 hours before pre-
paring recipe—it will be much easier to cut into
slices.

Jambalaya

2 1/2- to 3-pound broiler-fryer chicken,
  cut up
2 cups water
1 1/2 teaspoons salt
1/4 teaspoon pepper
8 pork sausage links
1 cup uncooked regular rice
1 medium onion, chopped (about 1/2 cup)
1/2 teaspoon dried thyme leaves
1/8 to 1/4 teaspoon cayenne pepper
1 large clove garlic, finely chopped
1 can (16 ounces) stewed tomatoes,
  undrained
Snipped parsley

Remove skin from chicken, if desired. Place
chicken, water, salt and pepper in Dutch oven.
Heat to boiling; reduce heat. Cover and simmer
20 minutes. Remove chicken from broth. Skim
fat from broth; strain broth.

Cook sausage links in Dutch oven until brown.
Drain fat, reserving 1 tablespoon in Dutch
oven. Add chicken; stir in broth and remaining
ingredients except parsley. Heat to boiling,
stirring once or twice; reduce heat. Cover and
simmer until thickest pieces of chicken are done
and rice is tender, 30 to 40 minutes. Sprinkle
with parsley.

Lemon Chicken

Vegetable oil
1/4 cup all-purpose flour
1/4 cup water
2 tablespoons cornstarch
2 tablespoons vegetable oil
1 teaspoon salt
1 teaspoon soy sauce
1/4 teaspoon baking soda
1 egg
3 medium whole chicken breasts (about 2 pounds), boned, skinned and cut into halves
Lemon Sauce (below)
1/2 lemon, thinly sliced

LEMON SAUCE

1/2 cup water
1/2 teaspoon grated lemon peel
1/4 cup lemon juice
1/4 cup honey
1 tablespoon catsup
1/2 teaspoon instant chicken bouillon
1/2 teaspoon salt
1 clove garlic, finely chopped
1 tablespoon cornstarch
1 tablespoon cold water

Heat oil (1 to 1 1/2 inches) to 360°. Beat remaining ingredients except chicken, Lemon Sauce and lemon slices with hand beater until smooth. Dip chicken pieces, one at a time, into batter. Fry 2 pieces at a time, turning once, until golden brown, about 7 minutes; drain.

Cut chicken crosswise into 1/2-inch slices. Arrange in single layer on warm platter; keep warm. Prepare Lemon Sauce; pour over chicken. Garnish with lemon slices.

Heat 1/2 cup water, the lemon peel, lemon juice, honey, catsup, bouillon (dry), salt and garlic to boiling. Mix cornstarch and 1 tablespoon water; stir into sauce. Cook and stir until thickened, about 30 seconds.

Note: After frying, chicken can be covered and refrigerated no longer than 24 hours. To serve, heat chicken on ungreased cookie sheet in 400° oven until hot, 10 to 12 minutes. Cut crosswise into 1/2-inch slices.

Chicken with Golden Pilaf

2 tablespoons vegetable oil
2 1/2- to 3-pound broiler-fryer chicken,
    cut up
1 teaspoon salt
2 medium carrots
1 medium onion, chopped (about 1/2 cup)
1/4 cup margarine or butter
2 1/4 cups water
1 cup uncooked regular rice
1/2 cup raisins
1 tablespoon instant chicken bouillon
1/2 teaspoon curry powder
1/4 teaspoon salt
1/4 teaspoon dried thyme leaves
1/4 cup toasted slivered almonds

Heat oil in 12-inch skillet or Dutch oven until hot. Cook chicken in oil over medium heat until brown, about 15 minutes; reduce heat. Drain fat from skillet. Sprinkle chicken with 1 teaspoon salt. Cover and cook over low heat until thickest pieces are done, 30 to 40 minutes. (Add 1 to 3 tablespoons water if necessary.) Uncover during last 5 minutes of cooking to crisp chicken.

Cut carrots lengthwise into 1/4-inch strips; cut into 1-inch pieces. Cook and stir onion in margarine in 2-quart saucepan until tender. Add carrots, water, rice, raisins, bouillon (dry), curry powder, 1/4 teaspoon salt and the thyme. Heat to boiling, stirring once or twice; reduce heat. Cover and simmer 14 minutes. (Do not lift cover or stir.) Remove from heat; fluff rice lightly with fork. Cover and let steam 5 to 10 minutes. Serve chicken with rice; top with almonds.

Chicken with Artichokes and Grapes

2 1/2- to 3-pound broiler-fryer chicken
6 slices bacon, cut up
1/2 teaspoon salt
1/2 teaspoon paprika
1/2 teaspoon dried tarragon leaves
1/2 cup dry white wine or apple juice
4 ounces mushrooms, sliced (about 1 1/2
    cups) or 1 can (4 ounces) mushroom
    stems and pieces, drained
1 can (14 ounces) artichoke hearts,
    drained and cut into halves
2 cups seedless green or red grapes
1 tablespoon cornstarch
2 tablespoons cold water

Cut chicken into pieces; cut each breast half into halves and remove skin. Fry bacon in 4-quart Dutch oven until crisp. Remove with slotted spoon and drain; reserve. Pour off all but 2 tablespoons bacon fat. Mix salt, paprika and tarragon; sprinkle over chicken. Cook chicken in bacon fat until light brown on all sides; add wine and mushrooms. Heat to boiling; reduce heat. Cover and simmer until thickest pieces are done, about 40 minutes. Remove chicken; keep warm. Add artichokes and grapes to Dutch oven; heat to boiling. Mix cornstarch and cold water; stir into artichoke mixture. Heat to boiling, stirring constantly. Boil and stir 1 minute. Pour over chicken; sprinkle with bacon.

Paella

2 tablespoons olive or vegetable oil
5 chicken drumsticks or 1 ½ pounds
  chicken pieces
6 ounces garlic-seasoned smoked pork
  sausage (chorizo)*
1 medium onion, chopped (about ½ cup)
1 clove garlic, crushed
3 cups Chicken Broth (page 8)
1 ½ cups uncooked regular rice
1 teaspoon salt
¼ teaspoon pepper
⅛ teaspoon cayenne pepper
⅛ teaspoon powdered saffron or ground
  turmeric
1 can (16 ounces) whole tomatoes,
  undrained
1 package (10 ounces) frozen cut green
  beans or green peas, thawed and
  drained
5 mussels or clams in shells

Heat oil in 12-inch skillet or Dutch oven until hot. Cook chicken in oil over medium heat until brown, about 15 minutes. Remove chicken from skillet. Remove casing from sausage; cut sausage into ½-inch slices. Cook and stir sausage, onion and garlic in skillet until sausage is light brown, about 5 minutes. Drain fat from skillet.

Stir broth, rice, salt, pepper, cayenne pepper, saffron and tomatoes into skillet; break up tomatoes with fork. Add chicken. Heat to boiling; reduce heat. Cover and simmer 20 minutes.

Stir in beans; cover and simmer until beans are almost tender, 5 to 10 minutes. Wash mussels thoroughly, discarding any broken-shell or open (dead) mussels. Add mussels to broth mixture; cover and simmer until mussels partially open, 5 to 7 minutes. Garnish with pimiento strips, if desired.

*Chorizo is a highly seasoned pork sausage with ground red pepper, pimiento, garlic and paprika added. Three-fourths to 1 cup cut-up fully cooked smoked ham can be substituted for the chorizo.

Chicken Curry

1/3 cup margarine or butter
1 1/2 teaspoons curry powder
1 small onion, coarsely chopped
1 clove garlic, chopped
1/4 cup all-purpose flour
2 teaspoons sugar
1/2 teaspoon ground ginger
1/4 teaspoon dry mustard
1/4 teaspoon pepper
1 medium tomato, chopped
1 medium tart apple, chopped
4 ounces fully cooked smoked ham, chopped
1/4 cup shredded coconut
2 cups Chicken Broth (page 8)
2 pounds chicken thighs and breasts, skinned, boned and cut into 1/2-inch slices
4 cups hot cooked rice
Condiments*

Cook and stir margarine, curry powder, onion and garlic in 3-quart saucepan until onion is transparent. Stir in flour, sugar, ginger, mustard, pepper, tomato, apple and ham. Cook, stirring occasionally, 5 minutes. Stir in coconut and broth. Heat to boiling; reduce heat. Cover and simmer, stirring occasionally, 1 hour.

Rub mixture through sieve. Return liquid to saucepan; add chicken. Heat to boiling; reduce heat. Cover and simmer until chicken is tender, 25 to 30 minutes. Serve with rice and, if desired, condiments.

*Shredded coconut, chopped peanuts, finely chopped hard-cooked eggs, chutney, finely chopped crystallized ginger, snipped parsley or raisins.

Couscous

2 tablespoons olive or vegetable oil
2 1/2- to 3-pound broiler-fryer chicken,
   cut up
2 teaspoons ground coriander
1 1/2 teaspoons salt
1 teaspoon instant chicken bouillon
1/4 teaspoon cayenne pepper
1/4 teaspoon ground turmeric
4 small carrots, cut into 2-inch pieces
2 medium onions, sliced
2 medium turnips, each cut into fourths
2 cloves garlic, finely chopped
1 cup water
3 small zucchini, cut into 1/4-inch slices
1 can (about 16 ounces) garbanzo beans
   (chickpeas), drained
Couscous (below)

Heat oil in Dutch oven until hot. Cook chicken in oil over medium heat until brown, about 15 minutes. Drain fat from Dutch oven. Add coriander, salt, bouillon (dry), cayenne pepper, turmeric, carrots, onions, turnips, garlic and water. Heat to boiling; reduce heat. Cover and simmer 30 minutes.

Add zucchini to chicken mixture. Cover and cook until thickest pieces of chicken are done and vegetables are tender, about 10 minutes. Add beans; heat 5 minutes.

Prepare Couscous. Mound on center of warm platter; arrange chicken and vegetables around Couscous.

COUSCOUS

1 1/3 cups couscous (semolina wheat
   cereal)
3/4 cup raisins
1/2 teaspoon salt
1 cup boiling water
1/2 cup margarine or butter
1/2 teaspoon ground turmeric

Mix couscous, raisins and salt in 2-quart bowl; stir in boiling water. Let stand until all water is absorbed, 2 to 3 minutes. Heat margarine in 10-inch skillet until melted; stir in couscous and turmeric. Cook over medium heat, stirring occasionally, 4 minutes.

Chicken with Lentils

4 slices bacon, cut into 2-inch pieces
2 1/2- to 3-pound broiler-fryer chicken
1 cup lentils
1 large stalk celery, sliced (about 3/4 cup)
1 medium onion, chopped (about 1/2 cup)
1 large clove garlic, finely chopped
1/2 cup dry white wine
1 can (16 ounces) whole tomatoes
1 teaspoon salt
1/2 teaspoon dried thyme leaves
1 tablespoon snipped parsley

Fry bacon in 12-inch skillet or 4-quart Dutch oven until crisp. Remove with slotted spoon and drain; reserve. Cut chicken into pieces; cut each breast half into halves and remove skin. Cook chicken in bacon fat over medium heat until light brown on all sides; remove chicken from skillet. Add lentils, celery, onion, garlic, wine, tomatoes (with liquid), salt, thyme and reserved bacon to skillet. Break up tomatoes with fork. Place chicken on mixture. Heat to boiling; reduce heat. Cover and cook until chicken is done and lentils are tender, about 45 minutes; sprinkle with parsley.

Chicken with Yogurt

1/4 cup sliced almonds
1 tablespoon margarine or butter
8 chicken drumsticks (about 2 pounds)
1 tablespoon margarine or butter
1/2 teaspoon paprika
1/4 teaspoon salt
1/4 teaspoon dried dill weed
1/3 cup water
1 teaspoon instant chicken bouillon
1 medium onion, sliced
1/2 cup plain yogurt
1 1/2 teaspoons cornstarch
1/4 cup cold water

Cook and stir almonds in 1 tablespoon margarine in 10-inch skillet over medium heat until almonds are golden brown. Remove with slotted spoon; drain and reserve.

Remove skin from chicken drumsticks. Cook drumsticks in 1 tablespoon margarine over medium heat until brown on all sides; reduce heat. Sprinkle with paprika, salt and dill weed. Mix 1/3 cup water and the bouillon (dry); pour over chicken. Add onion. Cover and simmer until drumsticks are done, about 30 minutes. Remove drumsticks; keep warm. Stir yogurt into liquid in skillet. Mix cornstarch and 1/4 cup cold water; gradually stir into yogurt mixture. Heat to boiling, stirring constantly. Boil and stir 1 minute. Pour yogurt sauce over drumsticks; sprinkle with almonds.

Following pages: Couscous

Chicken Paprika

2 tablespoons vegetable oil
2 1/2- to 3-pound broiler-fryer chicken,
   cut up
2 medium onions, chopped
1 clove garlic, chopped
1/2 cup water
2 tablespoons paprika
1 teaspoon salt
1/2 teaspoon instant chicken bouillon
1/4 teaspoon pepper
1 medium tomato, chopped
1 green pepper, cut into 1/2-inch strips
1 cup dairy sour cream

Heat oil in 12-inch skillet until hot. Cook chicken in oil over medium heat until brown on all sides, about 15 minutes; remove chicken. Cook and stir onions and garlic in oil until onions are tender; drain fat from skillet. Stir water, paprika, salt, bouillon (dry), pepper and tomato into skillet; loosen brown particles from bottom of skillet. Add chicken. Heat to boiling; reduce heat. Cover and simmer 20 minutes. Add green pepper; cover and cook until thickest pieces of chicken are done, 10 to 15 minutes longer.

Remove chicken; keep warm. Skim fat from skillet. Stir sour cream into liquid in skillet. Heat just until hot. Serve with chicken.

Chicken Chili

2 cups cut-up cooked chicken
1 large onion, chopped (about 1 cup)
1 medium green pepper, chopped (about
   1 cup)
3 to 4 teaspoons chili powder
1 teaspoon salt
1/4 teaspoon ground cumin
1/8 teaspoon red pepper sauce
2 cloves garlic, crushed
1 can (16 ounces) whole tomatoes,
   undrained
1 can (15 1/2 ounces) kidney beans,
   undrained
1 can (8 ounces) tomato sauce

Heat all ingredients to boiling in 3-quart saucepan; reduce heat. Cover and simmer, stirring occasionally, 20 to 30 minutes. Sprinkle with snipped parsley, if desired.

Note: To prepare ahead, omit kidney beans. After simmering mixture, cool quickly and pour into 5- to 6-cup freezer container; cover, label and freeze. About 1 hour before serving, dip container into very hot water just to loosen. Drain kidney beans, reserving liquid. Place reserved bean liquid and frozen block in saucepan. Cover and heat over medium heat, turning block occasionally, until mixture is hot, about 40 minutes. Stir in kidney beans; heat until hot.

Chicken with Asparagus Béarnaise

Béarnaise Sauce (below)
1 package (10 ounces) frozen asparagus
   spears
1 large whole chicken breast (about 1
   pound), boned, skinned and cut into
   fourths, or 4 chicken thighs, boned and
   skinned
2 tablespoons all-purpose flour
1/4 teaspoon salt
1/8 teaspoon pepper
2 tablespoons margarine or butter

BÉARNAISE SAUCE

3 egg yolks
1 tablespoon lemon juice
1/2 cup firm butter*
1 tablespoon dry white wine
1 tablespoon finely chopped onion
1 teaspoon dried tarragon leaves
1/2 teaspoon dried chervil leaves

Prepare Béarnaise Sauce. Cook asparagus as directed on package; drain. Place chicken between 2 pieces of waxed paper or plastic wrap; pound until 1/4 inch thick. Mix flour, salt and pepper; coat chicken.

Heat margarine in 10-inch skillet over medium heat until melted. Cook chicken in margarine until light brown and done, 3 to 4 minutes on each side. Place chicken on warm platter. Top each piece with asparagus. Top each serving with sauce.

Stir egg yolks and lemon juice vigorously in 1-quart saucepan. Add 1/4 cup of the butter. Heat over very low heat, stirring constantly, until butter is melted. Add remaining butter. Cook, stirring vigorously, until butter is melted and sauce thickens. (Be sure butter melts slowly because this gives eggs time to cook and thicken sauce without curdling.) Stir in remaining ingredients.

*We do not recommend margarine for this recipe.

Following pages: Chicken and Asparagus Béarnaise

· 3 ·

OVEN ALL-STARS

Country Broiled Chicken

6 SERVINGS

2 1/2-pound broiler-fryer chicken, cut up
1/2 cup margarine or butter
1/4 cup vegetable oil
2 tablespoons lemon juice
2 teaspoons salt
2 teaspoons sugar
1/2 teaspoon paprika
1/2 teaspoon ground ginger
1 small onion, finely chopped (about 1/4 cup)
1 medium clove garlic, crushed

Place chicken, skin sides down, on rack in broiler pan. Heat remaining ingredients, stirring occasionally, until margarine is melted; brush on chicken.

Set oven control to broil and/or 550°. Place broiler pan so top of chicken is 5 to 7 inches from heat. Brush with margarine mixture every 10 to 15 minutes and turn chicken as it browns; broil until thickest pieces are done, 40 to 50 minutes.

Broiled Pepper Chicken

7 SERVINGS

2 1/2- to 3-pound broiler-fryer chicken
1 tablespoon vegetable oil
2 teaspoons dried marjoram leaves
1 to 1 1/2 teaspoons red pepper flakes
2 teaspoons margarine or butter, melted
1/2 teaspoon salt

Cut chicken into pieces; cut each breast half into halves. Mix oil, marjoram, red pepper, margarine and salt; brush chicken on both sides with margarine mixture. Place chicken, skin sides down, on rack in broiler pan. Set oven control to broil and/or 550°. Broil chicken with tops 7 to 9 inches from heat 30 minutes; turn. Broil until brown and thickest pieces are done, 20 to 30 minutes longer.

Oven-fried Chicken

6 OR 7 SERVINGS

1/4 cup margarine, butter or vegetable oil
1/3 cup all-purpose flour
1 teaspoon salt
3/4 teaspoon paprika
1/4 teaspoon pepper
2 1/2- to 3-pound broiler-fryer chicken,
  cut up

Heat margarine in rectangular pan, 13 × 9 × 2 inches, in 400° oven until melted. Mix flour, salt, paprika and pepper; coat chicken. Place chicken, skin sides down, in pan; turn chicken to coat with margarine. Turn skin sides up. Cook uncovered until thickest pieces are done, 50 to 60 minutes.

CRUSTY CURRIED CHICKEN: Omit paprika; mix in 2 teaspoons curry powder with the flour.

OVEN-FRIED CHICKEN BREASTS: Substitute 6 small chicken breast halves for the broiler-fryer chicken. Cook 35 to 45 minutes.

Oven-fried Chicken with Herb Biscuits

6 OR 7 SERVINGS

1 tablespoon margarine or butter
1/2 cup variety baking mix
1 teaspoon salt
1 teaspoon paprika
1/4 teaspoon pepper
2 1/2- to 3-pound broiler-fryer chicken,
  cut up
Herb Biscuit Dough (below)
1 can (16 ounces) peach halves, drained

Heat margarine in rectangular pan, 13 × 9 × 2 inches, in 425° oven until melted. Mix baking mix, salt, paprika and pepper; coat chicken. Place chicken, skin sides down, in pan. Cook uncovered 35 minutes.

Prepare Herb Biscuit Dough. Turn chicken, pushing pieces to one side of pan. Drop dough by spoonfuls into pan in single layer next to chicken. Arrange peach halves on chicken. Cook uncovered until biscuits are light brown and thickest pieces of chicken are done, about 15 minutes.

HERB BISCUIT DOUGH

2 cups variety baking mix
2/3 cup milk
1 1/4 teaspoons caraway seed
1/2 teaspoon dried sage leaves
1/4 teaspoon dry mustard

Mix all ingredients until soft dough forms; beat vigorously 30 seconds.

Following pages: Cornmeal Chicken with Casera Sauce

Cornmeal Chicken

2 1/2- to 3-pound broiler-fryer chicken
2 tablespoons yellow cornmeal
1/8 teaspoon salt
1/2 teaspoon chili powder
1/4 teaspoon dried oregano leaves
2 tablespoons margarine or butter
2 tablespoons vegetable oil
Casera Sauce (below)

Cut chicken into pieces; cut each breast half into halves and remove skin. Mix cornmeal, salt, chili powder and oregano. Coat chicken with cornmeal mixture. Heat margarine and oil in rectangular pan, 13 × 9 × 2 inches, in 375° oven until margarine is melted. Place chicken, meaty sides down, in pan. Cook uncovered 30 minutes. Turn chicken; cook until brown and thickest pieces are done, 20 to 30 minutes longer. Prepare Casera Sauce; serve with chicken.

CASERA SAUCE

1 medium tomato, finely chopped
1 small onion, chopped (about 1/4 cup)
1 small clove garlic, crushed
1 canned green chili or jalapeño pepper, seeded and finely chopped
2 teaspoons finely snipped cilantro or parsley
2 teaspoons lemon juice
1/4 teaspoon dried oregano leaves

Mix all ingredients.

Baked Chicken with Herbs

2 1/2- to 3-pound broiler-fryer chicken
2 tablespoons margarine or butter
2 tablespoons olive or vegetable oil
1/4 cup finely chopped onion
1/4 cup lemon juice
2 tablespoons Worcestershire sauce
1/2 teaspoon dried basil leaves
1/4 teaspoon dried marjoram leaves
1/4 teaspoon dried oregano leaves
2 large cloves garlic, finely chopped

Cut chicken into pieces; cut each breast half into halves and remove skin. Heat margarine and oil in rectangular pan, 13 × 9 × 2 inches, in 375° oven until margarine is melted. Stir in remaining ingredients except chicken. Place chicken, meaty sides down, in pan, turning to coat with herb mixture. Cook uncovered 30 minutes. Turn chicken; cook until thickest pieces are done, about 30 minutes longer.

Wheat-stuffed Drumsticks

4 SERVINGS

¾ cup uncooked bulgur (cracked wheat)
¾ cup cold water
⅓ cup chopped green onions (with tops)
¼ teaspoon salt
¼ teaspoon ground sage
⅛ teaspoon pepper
8 chicken drumsticks (about 2 pounds)
2 tablespoons margarine or butter
2 tablespoons vegetable oil
½ cup whole wheat or all-purpose flour
1 teaspoon paprika
½ teaspoon salt
¼ teaspoon ground sage
¼ teaspoon pepper

Cover bulgur with cold water. Let stand 1 hour. Mix bulgur, onions, ¼ teaspoon salt, ¼ teaspoon sage and ⅛ teaspoon pepper. Carefully separate skin from meat all around each chicken drumstick, beginning at wide end. Fill opening with wheat mixture. Wipe off excess filling on outside of drumstick. Heat margarine and oil in rectangular pan, 13 × 9 × 2 inches, in 375° oven until margarine is melted. Mix remaining ingredients. Coat drumsticks with flour mixture; place in pan. Bake uncovered 30 minutes. Turn drumsticks; bake until done, about 30 minutes longer.

Glazed Chicken Drumsticks

8 SERVINGS

2 pounds chicken drumsticks
3 tablespoons soy sauce
2 tablespoons honey
1 tablespoon vegetable oil
1 tablespoon chili sauce
½ teaspoon salt
¼ teaspoon ground ginger
⅛ teaspoon garlic powder

Place drumsticks in ungreased baking dish. Mix remaining ingredients; pour over drumsticks. Cover and refrigerate at least 1 hour.

Line broiler pan with aluminum foil. Place drumsticks on rack in broiler pan. Brush drumsticks with remaining sauce. Cook in 375° oven until done, 50 to 60 minutes.

Following pages: Glazed Chicken Drumsticks

Oven-barbecued Chicken

2 1/2- to 3-pound broiler-fryer chicken
3/4 cup chili sauce
2 tablespoons honey
2 tablespoons soy sauce
1 teaspoon dry mustard
1/2 teaspoon prepared horseradish
1/2 teaspoon red pepper sauce

Cut chicken into pieces; cut each breast half into halves. Place chicken pieces, skin sides up, in ungreased rectangular pan, 13 × 9 × 2 inches. Mix remaining ingredients; pour over chicken. Cover and cook in 375° oven 30 minutes. Spoon sauce over chicken; cook uncovered until thickest pieces are done, about 30 minutes longer.

Chicken in Potato Shells

3 large hot baked potatoes
1 tablespoon margarine or butter, melted
2 cups cut-up cooked chicken
1 can (16 ounces) whole tomatoes, undrained
1 envelope (about 1 1/4 ounces) taco seasoning mix
1/2 cup shredded Cheddar or Monterey Jack cheese (2 ounces)
1/3 cup dairy sour cream
2 green onions (with tops), sliced

Heat oven to 475°. Cut each potato lengthwise into halves. Scoop out potatoes, leaving a 1/4-inch shell. (Use potatoes as desired.) Brush outsides and insides of shells with margarine. Place shells, cut sides up, on ungreased cookie sheet. Bake uncovered until edges are brown, 15 to 20 minutes.

Mix chicken, tomatoes and seasoning mix in 10-inch skillet; break up tomatoes. Heat to boiling; reduce heat. Simmer uncovered, stirring occasionally, 20 minutes. Spoon chicken mixture into shells; sprinkle with cheese. Heat just until cheese is melted. Top each with dollop of sour cream and sprinkle with green onions.

Note: To prepare ahead, bake potatoes and prepare shells as above. Cover and refrigerate no longer than 24 hours. Bake shells as directed.

Tandoori-style Chicken

8 chicken breast halves (about 4
   pounds), skinned and boned
1/2 teaspoon water
1/4 teaspoon dry mustard
1 cup plain yogurt
1/4 cup lemon juice
1 1/2 teaspoons salt
1 1/2 teaspoons paprika
1/2 teaspoon ground cardamom
1/2 teaspoon each red and yellow food
   color, if desired
1/4 teaspoon ground ginger
1/4 teaspoon ground cumin
1/4 teaspoon crushed dried red pepper
1/4 teaspoon pepper
1 clove garlic, crushed

Place chicken in glass bowl. Mix water and mustard; stir in remaining ingredients. Pour over chicken; turn to coat well. Cover and refrigerate at least 12 hours but no longer than 24 hours. Remove chicken from marinade; place chicken in ungreased baking dish, 13 × 9 × 2 inches. Bake uncovered in 375° oven until done, about 45 minutes.

Tarragon Chicken

6 small chicken breast halves (about 2
   pounds)
1/2 teaspoon paprika
6 small zucchini, cut lengthwise into
   halves, then into 2-inch pieces
4 medium carrots, cut into 1/4-inch slices
4 ounces small mushrooms
1/3 cup margarine or butter, melted
1 tablespoon lemon juice
1 teaspoon dried tarragon leaves
1/2 teaspoon salt
1/8 teaspoon pepper

Remove skin from chicken breasts. Place chicken, meaty sides up, in ungreased rectangular baking dish, 13 × 9 × 2 inches; sprinkle with paprika. Place zucchini, carrots and mushrooms around and over chicken. Mix remaining ingredients; drizzle over chicken and vegetables. Cover and cook in 350° oven until chicken is done, 50 to 60 minutes.

Garlic Chicken Breasts

1/4 cup margarine or butter, softened
1 tablespoon snipped chives or parsley
1/8 teaspoon garlic powder
6 small chicken breast halves (about 2
    pounds)
3 cups cornflakes cereal, crushed (about
    1 1/2 cups)
2 tablespoons snipped parsley
1/2 teaspoon paprika
1/4 cup buttermilk or milk

Mix margarine, chives and garlic powder; shape into rectangle, 3 × 2 inches. Cover and freeze until firm, about 30 minutes. Remove skin and bones from chicken breasts. Flatten each chicken breast to 1/4-inch thickness between waxed paper or plastic wrap. Cut margarine mixture crosswise into 6 pieces. Place 1 piece on center of each chicken breast. Fold long sides over margarine; fold ends up and secure with wooden pick. Mix cereal, parsley and paprika. Dip chicken into buttermilk; coat evenly with cereal mixture. Place chicken breasts, seam sides down, in greased square pan, 9 × 9 × 2 inches. Cook uncovered in 425° oven until chicken is done, about 35 minutes.

Arroz con Pollo

2 1/2- to 3-pound broiler-fryer chicken,
    cut up
3/4 teaspoon salt
1/4 to 1/2 teaspoon paprika
1/4 teaspoon pepper
2 1/2 cups Chicken Broth (page 8)
1 cup uncooked regular rice
1 medium onion, chopped (about 1/2 cup)
1 teaspoon garlic salt
1/2 teaspoon dried oregano leaves
1/8 teaspoon ground turmeric
1 bay leaf, crumbled
1 package (10 ounces) frozen green peas,
    thawed and drained
Pimiento strips
Pitted ripe olives

Place chicken, skin sides up, in ungreased rectangular baking dish, 13 × 9 × 2 inches. Sprinkle with salt, paprika and pepper. Cook uncovered in 350° oven 30 minutes.

Heat broth to boiling. Remove chicken and drain fat from dish. Mix broth, rice, onion, garlic salt, oregano, turmeric, bay leaf and peas in baking dish. Top with chicken; cover with aluminum foil. Cook in oven until rice and thickest pieces of chicken are done and liquid is absorbed, about 30 minutes. Garnish with pimiento strips and olives.

Chicken Parmesan

Tomato Sauce (below)
6 large chicken thighs (about 1 1/2
    pounds)
1/3 cup all-purpose flour
1/4 teaspoon salt
1/8 teaspoon pepper
1/2 cup milk
1 egg, slightly beaten
1/2 cup dry bread crumbs
2 tablespoons olive or vegetable oil
1 cup shredded mozzarella cheese
1/4 cup grated Parmesan cheese

Prepare Tomato Sauce. Remove skin and bones from chicken thighs. Pound chicken thighs between waxed paper or plastic wrap to about 1/4-inch thickness. Mix flour, salt and pepper. Coat chicken with flour mixture. Mix milk and egg. Dip chicken into milk mixture; coat with bread crumbs. Heat oil in 10-inch skillet over medium heat until hot. Cook chicken, turning once, until golden brown (add oil to skillet if necessary). Place chicken in rectangular pan, 13 X 9 X 2 inches. Sprinkle with mozzarella cheese. Pour Tomato Sauce over cheese; sprinkle with Parmesan cheese. Cook uncovered in 375° oven until hot and bubbly, about 20 minutes.

TOMATO SAUCE

1 medium onion, chopped
2 large cloves garlic, crushed
1 tablespoon olive or vegetable oil
1 can (16 ounces) whole tomatoes,
    undrained
1 can (4 ounces) mushroom stems and
    pieces, drained and chopped
2 tablespoons red wine vinegar
1/2 teaspoon dried oregano leaves
1/2 teaspoon dried basil leaves
1/4 teaspoon dried marjoram leaves

Cook and stir onion and garlic in oil in 2-quart saucepan until onion is tender, about 5 minutes. Add remaining ingredients. Break up tomatoes with fork. Heat to boiling; reduce heat. Simmer uncovered, stirring occasionally, until thickened, about 10 minutes.

Following pages: Arroz con Pollo

Sweet-and-Sour Chicken

2 1/2- to 3-pound broiler-fryer chicken,
   cut up
3 tablespoons margarine or butter
2 tablespoons water
1 egg
1 cup variety baking mix
1/3 cup packed brown sugar
2 tablespoons cornstarch
1 can (15 1/2 ounces) pineapple chunks in
   syrup, drained (reserve syrup)
3 tablespoons vinegar
2 tablespoons catsup
2 tablespoons soy sauce
1 medium green pepper, cut into 1-inch
   pieces
1 small onion, thinly sliced
4 cups hot cooked rice

Remove bones and skin from chicken; cut chicken into 1-inch pieces. Heat margarine in rectangular pan, 13 × 9 × 2 inches, in 400° oven until melted. Beat water and egg slightly. Dip chicken into egg mixture, then coat with baking mix. Place chicken in pan. Cook uncovered in 400° oven until bottoms of chicken pieces are golden brown, 25 to 30 minutes. Turn chicken; cook until done, 10 to 15 minutes longer.

Mix brown sugar and cornstarch in 3-quart saucepan. Add enough water to reserved pineapple syrup to measure 1⅔ cups. Stir syrup mixture, vinegar, catsup and soy sauce into saucepan. Cook over medium-high heat, stirring constantly, until mixture thickens and boils. Stir in pineapple, green pepper and onion; reduce heat. Cover and simmer until green pepper is crisp-tender, 5 to 7 minutes. Stir in chicken; heat thoroughly. Serve over rice.

Chicken Teriyaki

2 small whole chicken breasts (about 1
  pound), boned, skinned and cut into
  halves
¼ cup soy sauce
¼ cup vegetable oil
2 tablespoons white wine*
2 teaspoons chopped gingerroot or ½
  teaspoon ground ginger
1 teaspoon sugar
1 clove garlic, finely chopped

Place chicken in glass or plastic container. Mix remaining ingredients; pour over chicken. Cover and refrigerate, turning occasionally, at least 1 hour.

Set oven control to broil and/or 550°. Place chicken on rack in broiler pan. Broil with tops about 4 inches from heat 5 minutes; turn chicken. Brush with marinade; broil until chicken is done, 5 to 6 minutes longer. Place on warm platter. Serve with cooked rice, if desired.

*Apple juice, pineapple juice, orange juice or water can be substituted for the wine.

Chicken and Dressing Casserole

2 tablespoons vegetable oil
⅓ cup all-purpose flour
1 teaspoon salt
½ teaspoon paprika
¼ teaspoon pepper
2½- to 3-pound broiler-fryer chicken,
  cut up
1 can (10¾ ounces) condensed cream of
  chicken or cream of mushroom soup
6 cups soft bread cubes
1 cup milk
¾ cup chopped celery
1 medium onion, chopped (about ½ cup)
¼ cup margarine or butter, melted
1 teaspoon salt
½ teaspoon ground sage
½ teaspoon dried thyme leaves
¼ teaspoon pepper

Heat oil in 10-inch skillet until hot. Mix flour, 1 teaspoon salt, the paprika and ¼ teaspoon pepper; coat chicken. Cook chicken in oil over medium heat until brown, about 15 minutes. Place in ungreased 2½-quart casserole or rectangular baking dish, 13 × 9 × 2 inches. Pour soup over chicken.

Toss remaining ingredients. Mound mixture on chicken. Cover and cook in 350° oven until thickest pieces of chicken are done, 1 to 1¼ hours.

Chicken and Corn Casserole

6 SERVINGS

1 can (17 ounces) whole kernel corn,
  drained
2 cups cut-up cooked chicken
1/2 cup sliced ripe olives
1 can (10 3/4 ounces) condensed cream of
  chicken soup
1/2 cup dairy sour cream
1/2 teaspoon salt
1/2 teaspoon ground cumin
1 can (4 ounces) chopped green chilies,
  undrained
1 jar (2 ounces) diced pimientos,
  undrained
2 cups tortilla chips or potato chips,
  coarsely crushed (about 1 cup)

Place corn in ungreased 2-quart casserole or square baking dish, 8 × 8 × 2 inches. Top with chicken and olives. Mix remaining ingredients except tortilla chips; spread over chicken mixture. Sprinkle with chips. Cook uncovered in 350° oven until hot, about 45 minutes.

TO MICROWAVE: Prepare as directed in 2-quart microwavable casserole, except do not sprinkle with chips. Cover tightly and microwave on high (100%) 8 minutes; rotate casserole 1/2 turn. Cover and microwave until center is hot, 6 to 8 minutes longer. Sprinkle with chips.

CHICKEN AND HOMINY CASSEROLE: Substitute 1 can (20 ounces) hominy, drained, for the corn.

Spinach and Chicken Casserole

5 SERVINGS

3 cups soft bread cubes
1 cup cut-up cooked chicken
1 package (10 ounces) frozen chopped
  spinach, thawed and very well drained
3/4 cup dairy sour cream
1 can (4 ounces) mushroom stems and
  pieces, drained
2 tablespoons finely chopped onion
1 medium clove garlic, finely chopped
3/4 teaspoon salt
1/4 teaspoon dry mustard
3 eggs, separated
3 tablespoons margarine or butter,
  melted
1/2 teaspoon poppy seed

Heat oven to 350°. Mix 1 1/2 cups of the bread cubes, the chicken, spinach, sour cream, mushrooms, onion, garlic, salt, mustard and egg yolks. Beat egg whites until stiff but not dry; fold into chicken mixture. Pour into greased 1 1/2-quart casserole. Toss remaining bread cubes, the margarine and poppy seed; sprinkle over chicken mixture. Cook uncovered in 350° oven until center is set and top is golden, about 45 minutes.

Chicken with Apricots

2 1/2- to 3-pound broiler-fryer chicken
2 tablespoons soy sauce
2 tablespoons honey
1 tablespoon vegetable oil
1 tablespoon chili sauce
1/2 teaspoon ground ginger
1/8 teaspoon cayenne pepper
1 can (16 ounces) apricot halves in
  juice, drained

Cut chicken into pieces; cut each breast half into halves and remove skin. Place chicken in rectangular pan, 13 × 9 × 2 inches. Mix remaining ingredients except apricots; brush over chicken, turning pieces to coat. Cook uncovered in 375° oven, brushing with soy mixture occasionally, until thickest pieces are done, 50 to 60 minutes. About 5 minutes before chicken is done, arrange apricots around chicken; brush chicken and apricots with soy mixture. Cook until apricots are hot, about 5 minutes. Spoon liquid from pan over chicken and apricots.

Orange Chicken with Brown Rice

2 tablespoons vegetable oil
2 tablespoons margarine or butter
1/4 cup all-purpose flour
1/2 teaspoon salt
1/2 teaspoon paprika
1/8 teaspoon pepper
2 1/2- to 3-pound broiler-fryer chicken,
  cut up
4 cups cooked brown rice
1 medium onion, thinly sliced
1 small green pepper, chopped (about 1/2
  cup)
1 jar (4 1/2 ounces) sliced mushrooms,
  drained
1 cup orange juice
1/4 cup dry white wine or apple juice
1 tablespoon packed brown sugar
1 teaspoon salt

Heat oil and margarine in rectangular baking dish, 13 × 9 × 2 inches, in 425° oven until margarine is melted. Mix flour, 1/2 teaspoon salt, the paprika and pepper; coat chicken. Place chicken, skin sides down, in baking dish. Cook uncovered 30 minutes.

Remove chicken and drain fat from dish. Place rice in baking dish; arrange onion, green pepper and mushrooms on top. Arrange chicken, skin sides up, on vegetables. Mix remaining ingredients; pour over top. Cover and cook until thickest pieces of chicken are done, 20 to 30 minutes. Garnish with orange slices, if desired.

Mexican Chicken in Crust

Tortilla Crust (below)
3 to 4 cups cut-up cooked chicken
1 can (10¾ ounces) condensed cream of
*   chicken soup*
1 cup dairy sour cream
1 can (4 ounces) green chilies, drained,
*   seeded and chopped*
½ cup finely chopped onion
2 cups shredded Monterey Jack cheese (8
*   ounces)*
¼ cup sliced green onions (with tops)

Prepare Tortilla Crust; roll dough into rectangle, 20 × 13 inches. Fold rectangle crosswise into thirds. Place in ungreased rectangular baking dish, 11 × 7 × 1½ inches; unfold. Spread chicken over dough in dish.

Heat oven to 400°. Mix soup, sour cream, chilies and onion in 2-quart saucepan. Heat over medium heat, stirring occasionally, until hot; pour over chicken. Sprinkle with cheese and green onions. Fold ends of dough over filling to center of dish. Pinch ends of dough together at 7-inch sides of dish to seal. Cut slits in top to let steam escape. Bake until crust is golden brown, 45 to 50 minutes.

TORTILLA CRUST

⅓ cup shortening
2 cups all-purpose flour
1 teaspoon salt
¾ teaspoon baking powder
½ to ¾ cup warm water

Cut shortening into flour, salt and baking powder until mixture resembles fine crumbs. Stir in water with fork until dough leaves side of bowl and rounds up into a ball. Turn dough onto lightly floured surface. Knead until smooth, 10 to 12 times. Cover and let rest about 15 minutes.

Chicken and Artichoke Fondue

16 chicken thighs (about 4 pounds)
⅓ cup all-purpose flour
1 teaspoon salt
¼ teaspoon pepper
2 tablespoons margarine or butter
2 tablespoons vegetable oil
1 can (14 ounces) artichoke hearts,
   drained and cut into fourths
8 slices bacon, crisply fried and crumbled
Fondue Sauce (below)
Paprika

Remove skin and bones from chicken thighs. Mix flour, salt and pepper; coat chicken with flour mixture. Heat margarine and oil over medium heat in 12-inch skillet until margarine is melted. Cook half of the chicken, turning occasionally, until light brown, about 15 minutes. Repeat with remaining chicken. Arrange chicken in ungreased rectangular baking dish, 13 × 9 × 2 inches.

Place artichokes on chicken; sprinkle with bacon. Prepare Fondue Sauce; pour over bacon. Sprinkle with paprika. Bake uncovered in 350° oven until hot and bubbly, 30 to 35 minutes.

FONDUE SAUCE

3 tablespoons margarine or butter
3 tablespoons all-purpose flour
¼ teaspoon salt
Dash of pepper
Dash of ground nutmeg
1½ cups milk
⅓ cup dry white wine
1½ cups shredded Swiss cheese (6
   ounces)

Heat margarine in 1½-quart saucepan until melted. Blend in flour, salt, pepper and nutmeg. Cook over low heat, stirring constantly, until smooth and bubbly; remove from heat. Stir in milk and wine. Heat to boiling, stirring constantly. Boil and stir 1 minute; remove from heat. Stir in cheese until melted.

Note: Before cooking, casserole can be covered and refrigerated no longer than 24 hours.

Following pages: Mexican Chicken in Crust

Chicken and Wild Rice Casserole

Wild and White Rice (below)
1/4 cup margarine or butter
1/3 cup all-purpose flour
1 teaspoon salt
1/8 teaspoon pepper
1 1/2 cups milk
1 cup Chicken Broth (page 8)
2 cups cut-up cooked chicken
1/3 cup chopped green pepper
2 tablespoons slivered almonds
2 tablespoons chopped pimiento
1 can (4 ounces) mushroom stems and
  pieces, drained

WILD AND WHITE RICE

1/4 cup uncooked wild rice
2/3 cup water
1/2 teaspoon salt
1/4 cup uncooked regular white rice
1/2 cup water

Prepare Wild and White Rice. Heat margarine in 3-quart saucepan over low heat until melted. Stir in flour, salt and pepper. Cook, stirring constantly, until smooth and bubbly. Remove from heat; stir in milk and broth. Heat to boiling, stirring constantly. Boil and stir 1 minute. Stir in rice and remaining ingredients. Pour into ungreased 1 1/2-quart casserole. Cook uncovered in 350° oven until hot and bubbly, 40 to 45 minutes. Sprinkle top with snipped parsley, if desired.

Wash wild rice. Heat wild rice, 2/3 cup water and the salt to boiling in 1-quart saucepan; reduce heat. Cover and simmer 30 minutes. Add white rice and 1/2 cup water. Heat to boiling; reduce heat. Cover and simmer 15 minutes. Remove from heat. Fluff rice with fork; cover and let stand 5 minutes.

Note: Before cooking, casserole can be covered and refrigerated no longer than 24 hours.

TO MICROWAVE: Prepare Wild and White Rice as directed. Microwave margarine in 2-quart microwavable casserole on high (100%) until melted, about 45 seconds. Stir in flour, salt and pepper. Decrease milk to 1/2 cup. Stir broth and milk into flour mixture. Microwave, stirring every minute, until thickened, 4 to 5 minutes. Stir in rice and remaining ingredients. Cover and microwave until hot and bubbly, 5 to 8 minutes longer.

Chicken and Rice with Curry Sauce

6 OR 7 SERVINGS

1 can (20 ounces) sliced pineapple
1/4 cup soy sauce
2 teaspoons ground ginger
1/4 teaspoon pepper
2 1/2- to 3-pound broiler-fryer chicken, cut up
1/4 cup shortening
1/2 cup all-purpose flour
3 cups cooked rice
3/4 cup raisins
1/4 cup toasted chopped almonds
Curry Sauce (below)

Drain pineapple, reserving 1/3 cup syrup. Mix reserved pineapple syrup, the soy sauce, ginger and pepper. Place chicken in large glass dish; pour syrup mixture over top. Cover and refrigerate, turning chicken occasionally, no longer than 12 hours.

Heat shortening in 10-inch skillet until hot. Remove chicken from dish, reserving 3 tablespoons of the marinade. Coat chicken with flour. Cook chicken in shortening over medium heat until brown, about 15 minutes.

Mix rice, raisins and almonds in ungreased rectangular baking dish, 11 × 7 × 1 1/2 inches. Top with pineapple slices and chicken; sprinkle with reserved marinade. Cover and cook in 350° oven 40 minutes. Uncover and cook until thickest pieces of chicken are done, about 10 minutes longer. Serve with Curry Sauce.

CURRY SAUCE

1 tablespoon margarine or butter
1 tablespoon all-purpose flour
1 tablespoon instant minced onion
1/2 teaspoon curry powder
1/4 teaspoon ground ginger
1/8 teaspoon garlic powder
1 cup milk
1/4 cup toasted coconut*

Heat margarine in saucepan over low heat until melted. Stir in flour, onion, curry powder, ginger and garlic powder. Cook, stirring constantly, until bubbly. Remove from heat; stir in milk. Heat to boiling, stirring constantly. Boil and stir 1 minute. Stir in coconut; heat until hot.

*To toast coconut, place in baking pan in 350° oven, stirring frequently, until golden, about 5 minutes.

Chicken with Phyllo

1/4 cup margarine or butter
1/4 cup all-purpose flour
1 tablespoon dry mustard
1 teaspoon salt
1/4 teaspoon pepper
2 cups milk
1 package (8 ounces) cream cheese, cut into 1/2-inch pieces
1 package (10 ounces) frozen green peas
2 cups cut-up cooked chicken
2 medium stalks celery, sliced (about 1 cup)
1/2 cup sliced green onions (with tops)
6 frozen phyllo sheets, thawed
1/4 cup margarine or butter, melted

Heat 1/4 cup margarine in 3-quart saucepan over low heat until melted. Stir in flour, mustard, salt and pepper. Cook, stirring constantly, until smooth and bubbly. Remove from heat; stir in milk. Heat to boiling, stirring constantly. Boil and stir 1 minute. Remove from heat; stir in cream cheese. Beat until smooth.

Rinse frozen peas under running cold water to separate; drain. Stir peas, chicken, celery and onions into sauce. Spread in ungreased square baking dish, 8 × 8 × 2 inches.

Cut phyllo sheets crosswise into halves; cover with damp towel to keep them from drying out. Carefully separate 1 half-sheet; place on chicken mixture, folding edges under to fit dish if necessary. Brush with melted margarine. Repeat with remaining 11 half-sheets. Brush top with melted margarine. Cut top into 6 servings. Cook uncovered in 375° oven until golden brown, about 45 minutes. Let stand 10 minutes before serving.

Chicken-Sausage Pies

½ pound bulk pork sausage
Savory Pastry (below)
1 jar (2½ ounces) sliced mushrooms,
  drained (reserve liquid)
¼ cup margarine or butter
¼ cup all-purpose flour
¼ teaspoon salt
1 can (10¾ ounces) chicken broth (1⅔
  cups)
1 cup light cream
2 cups cut-up cooked chicken

Heat oven to 400°. Shape pork sausage into ½-inch balls. Place on rack in broiler pan and bake 15 minutes. Remove from oven and set aside.

Increase oven temperature to 425°. Prepare Savory Pastry and place pastry rounds on ungreased baking sheet; prick thoroughly with a fork. Bake 8 to 10 minutes or until golden brown.

Cook and stir mushrooms in butter 5 minutes. Stir in flour and salt and cook over low heat, stirring until mixture is bubbly. Immediately stir in broth, cream and the reserved liquid. Heat to boiling, stirring constantly. Boil and stir 1 minute.

Divide sausage balls and chicken among 6 ungreased casseroles. Pour cream sauce over meat. Top each casserole with baked pastry round. Heat in 425° oven until sauce bubbles.

SAVORY PASTRY

1 cup all-purpose flour
1 teaspoon celery seed
½ teaspoon salt
½ teaspoon paprika
⅓ cup plus 1 tablespoon shortening
2 to 3 tablespoons cold water

Measure flour, celery seed, salt and paprika into bowl. Cut in shortening thoroughly. Sprinkle in the water, 1 tablespoon at a time, mixing until dough almost cleans side of bowl.

Gather dough into ball and shape into flattened round. Roll about ⅛ inch thick on lightly floured, cloth-covered board. Cut into 6 rounds to fit tops of 1½-cup individual casseroles.

· 4 ·

WONDERFUL ROASTS

French Country-style Chicken

3- to 3 1/2-pound broiler-fryer chicken
2 tablespoons margarine or butter
1 can (10 3/4 ounces) condensed chicken
  broth
1 teaspoon salt
1/4 teaspoon pepper
1/4 teaspoon dried thyme leaves
8 medium carrots, each cut into fourths
8 small whole white onions, or 2 medium
  onions, each cut into fourths
4 medium turnips, each cut into fourths
1/2 cup dry white wine
2 tablespoons cold water
1 tablespoon cornstarch

Fold chicken wings across back with tips touching; tie drumsticks to tail. Heat margarine in Dutch oven over medium heat until melted. Cook chicken in margarine until brown on all sides, 20 to 30 minutes. Pour broth over chicken; sprinkle with salt, pepper and thyme. Cover and cook in 375° oven 45 minutes. Arrange carrots, onions and turnips around chicken. Cover and cook until thickest pieces of chicken are done, 1 to 1 1/2 hours.

Remove chicken and vegetables to warm platter; remove string. Keep chicken warm. Skim fat from chicken broth; stir wine into broth. Heat to boiling. Mix water and cornstarch; stir into broth. Heat to boiling, stirring constantly. Boil and stir 1 minute. Serve sauce with chicken.

Herbed Lemon Chicken

Stuffing (below)
2 1/2- to 3-pound broiler-fryer chicken
1/4 cup margarine or butter, melted
2 tablespoons lemon juice
1/2 teaspoon dried oregano leaves
1 small clove garlic, finely chopped

Prepare Stuffing. Fill wishbone area of chicken with stuffing first. Fasten neck skin to back with skewer. Fold wings across back with tips touching. Fill body cavity lightly. Tie or skewer drumsticks to tail. Place chicken, breast side up, on rack in shallow roasting pan. Mix remaining ingredients; generously brush over chicken. Roast uncovered in 375° oven, brushing with margarine mixture 2 or 3 times, until thickest parts are done and drumstick meat feels very soft, about 1 3/4 hours.

STUFFING

2 tablespoons lemon juice
Herbed Bread Stuffing (page 9)

Add lemon juice to prepared stuffing. Toss lightly to mix.

Autumn Roast Chicken

2 1/2- to 3-pound broiler-fryer chicken
1/2 cup margarine or butter, melted
1/4 cup lemon juice
2 tablespoons honey
2 teaspoons dried rosemary leaves,
    crushed
1 clove garlic, finely chopped
3 pounds winter squash, cut into 1-inch
    rings or slices
6 medium onions, cut into halves

Prepare chicken as directed in Roast Chicken (page 9). Place breast side up on rack in shallow roasting pan. Mix margarine, lemon juice, honey, rosemary and garlic. Arrange squash and onions around chicken. Brush chicken and vegetables with margarine mixture. Roast uncovered in 375° oven, brushing chicken and vegetables several times with remaining margarine mixture, until chicken and vegetables are done, about 1 1/2 hours.

Ginger Chicken with Vegetables

7 SERVINGS

2 1/2- to 3-pound whole broiler-fryer
  chicken
1/4 cup margarine or butter, melted
1/4 teaspoon paprika
1/4 teaspoon ground ginger
2 packages (6 ounces each) frozen pea
  pods
1 medium onion, chopped (about 1/2 cup)
1/2 teaspoon ground turmeric
1/4 teaspoon ground ginger
2 tablespoons margarine or butter
8 ounces medium mushrooms
1 teaspoon salt
2 teaspoons lemon juice
8 cherry tomatoes, cut into halves

Fold wings of chicken across back with tips touching. Tie drumsticks to tail. Place chicken, breast side up, on rack in shallow roasting pan. Mix 1/4 cup margarine, the paprika and 1/4 teaspoon ginger; generously brush over chicken. Roast uncovered in 375° oven, brushing with margarine mixture 2 or 3 times, until thickest parts are done and drumstick meat feels very soft, about 1 1/4 hours.

About 15 minutes before chicken is done, rinse pea pods under running cold water to separate; drain. Cook and stir onion, turmeric and 1/4 teaspoon ginger in 2 tablespoons margarine in 10-inch skillet over medium heat until onion is almost tender, about 3 minutes. Stir in pea pods, mushrooms, salt and lemon juice. Cook uncovered, stirring occasionally, until pea pods are hot, about 5 minutes. Stir in cherry tomatoes; heat just until hot. Serve vegetables with chicken.

Chicken with Gravy

7 SERVINGS

2 1/2- to 3-pound whole broiler-fryer
  chicken
1 tablespoon margarine or butter,
  softened
1/2 teaspoon salt
1/4 teaspoon ground allspice
1 tablespoon margarine or butter
1/4 cup water
Gravy (page 69)

Fold wings of chicken across back with tips touching. Tie drumsticks to tail. Mix softened margarine, salt and allspice; brush over chicken. Heat 1 tablespoon margarine in 4-quart Dutch oven over medium heat until melted. Cook chicken until brown on all sides; add water. Cover and cook, breast side up, over low heat until chicken is done, 30 to 40 minutes. Remove chicken; keep warm. Prepare Gravy; serve with chicken.

Milk

$^{1}/_{2}$ *cup milk*

$^{1}/_{4}$ *cup all-purpose flour*

$^{1}/_{2}$ *teaspoon salt*

$^{1}/_{8}$ *teaspoon ground allspice*

1 can (4 ounces) mushroom stems and pieces, drained

1 teaspoon currant jelly

Pour drippings into measuring cup; skim off any excess fat. Add enough milk to drippings to measure 1 $^{1}/_{2}$ cups; return to Dutch oven. Shake $^{1}/_{2}$ cup milk, the flour, salt and allspice in tightly covered container; gradually stir into drippings mixture. Stir in mushrooms and jelly. Heat to boiling, stirring constantly. Boil and stir 1 minute.

Rice-stuffed Chicken

7 SERVINGS

$^{1}/_{3}$ *cup margarine or butter, melted*

1 teaspoon salt

1 teaspoon ground ginger

$^{1}/_{2}$ *teaspoon finely shredded lemon peel*

$^{1}/_{4}$ *teaspoon garlic powder*

1 $^{1}/_{2}$ cups cooked brown or regular rice

1 medium apple, chopped (about 1 cup)

$^{1}/_{2}$ *cup chopped nuts*

$^{1}/_{2}$ *cup cut-up prunes*

$^{1}/_{2}$ *cup cut-up dried apricots*

$^{1}/_{4}$ *cup chopped celery*

2 $^{1}/_{2}$- to 3-pound whole broiler-fryer chicken

2 tablespoons margarine or butter, melted

$^{1}/_{4}$ *teaspoon paprika*

Mix $^{1}/_{3}$ cup margarine, the salt, ginger, lemon peel and garlic powder; toss with rice, apple, nuts, prunes, apricots and celery. Fill wishbone area of chicken with stuffing first. Fasten neck skin to back with skewer. Fold wings across back with tips touching. Fill body cavity lightly. (Place any remaining stuffing in small ungreased baking dish; cover and refrigerate. Place in oven with chicken the last 30 minutes of roasting.) Tie or skewer drumsticks to tail. Place chicken, breast side up, on rack in shallow roasting pan. Mix 2 tablespoons margarine and the paprika; brush over chicken. Roast uncovered in 375° oven until thickest parts are done and drumstick meat feels very soft, 1 $^{1}/_{4}$ to 1 $^{3}/_{4}$ hours.

Following pages: Ginger Chicken with Vegetables

Cornish Hens with Glazed Oranges

6 SERVINGS

3 Rock Cornish hens (about 1 1/2 pounds each)
2 tablespoons margarine or butter, melted
Glazed Oranges (below)
1/2 cup orange juice
1 tablespoon honey
1/2 teaspoon salt
1/4 teaspoon dry mustard
1/8 teaspoon paprika

Place hens, breast sides up, on rack in shallow roasting pan; brush with margarine. Roast uncovered in 350° oven 30 minutes.

Prepare Glazed Oranges. Mix remaining ingredients; brush half of the orange juice mixture over hens. Roast uncovered, brushing with remaining orange juice mixture, until hens are done, about 45 minutes longer. Cut each hen along backbone from tail to neck into halves with kitchen scissors. Serve with Glazed Oranges.

GLAZED ORANGES

3 medium oranges
2 tablespoons margarine or butter
1/4 cup light corn syrup
1 tablespoon honey

Cut off ends of oranges; cut each orange into 1/8-inch slices. Heat margarine in 12-inch skillet over medium heat until melted. Stir in corn syrup and honey. Heat to boiling; add oranges and reduce heat. Simmer uncovered, spooning sauce frequently over oranges, until oranges are tender and glazed, about 25 minutes.

Savory Rock Cornish Hens

4 Rock Cornish hens (1 to 1 1/4 pounds
  each)
Salt
Melted margarine or butter
1 cup uncooked wild rice
1 can (10 3/4 ounces) chicken broth
Water
1/2 teaspoon salt
2/3 cup raisins
2/3 cup orange juice
1/4 cup margarine or butter
1/4 cup all-purpose flour
1 teaspoon salt
1/4 teaspoon paprika
1/8 teaspoon pepper
2 cups milk

Thaw hens if frozen. Heat oven to 350°. Wash hens and pat dry. If desired, rub cavities lightly with salt. Place hens breast side up on rack in open shallow roasting pan; brush with melted margarine. Do not add water. Do not cover. Roast 50 minutes, brushing hens 3 or 4 times with the melted margarine.

While hens roast, wash rice thoroughly; drain. Into large saucepan, measure broth and enough water to measure 3 cups liquid. Add rice and 1/2 teaspoon salt. Heat to boiling, stirring once or twice. Reduce heat; cover tightly and simmer about 45 minutes or until all liquid is absorbed and rice is tender.

Increase oven temperature to 400°; roast hens 10 minutes longer or until brown. Combine raisins and orange juice in small saucepan; heat to boiling. Reduce heat and simmer 5 minutes; set aside.

Melt 1/4 cup margarine in small saucepan. Blend in flour, 1 teaspoon salt, the paprika and pepper. Cook over low heat, stirring until mixture is smooth and bubbly. Remove from heat; stir in milk. Heat to boiling, stirring constantly. Boil and stir 1 minute. Gradually stir in raisin-orange juice mixture.

Place hens on bed of hot wild rice; pour some of the raisin sauce over hens. Serve remaining sauce separately.

Following pages: Cornish Hens with Glazed Oranges

· 5 ·

SALADS FOR ALL SEASONS

Club Salad

4 OR 5 SERVINGS

Barbecue Salad Dressing (below)
2 cups cut-up cooked chicken
5 slices bacon, crisply fried and crumbled
2 heads Bibb or Boston lettuce or 1 head
* iceberg lettuce, torn into bite-size*
* pieces*
2 medium tomatoes, cut into wedges
1 hard-cooked egg, peeled and sliced

Prepare Barbecue Salad Dressing. Toss remaining ingredients except egg slices. Garnish with egg slices; serve with dressing.

BARBECUE SALAD DRESSING

½ cup mayonnaise or salad dressing
¼ cup barbecue sauce
1 tablespoon instant minced onion
1 tablespoon lemon juice
½ teaspoon salt
¼ teaspoon pepper

Mix all ingredients; cover and refrigerate.

Chicken Salad with Honey Dressing

6 SERVINGS

Honey Dressing (below)
3 cups cut-up cooked chicken
1½ cups seedless grapes
¼ cup sliced green onions (with tops)
¼ cup chopped green pepper
1 can (8 ounces) water chestnuts,
    drained and chopped
2 oranges, pared and sectioned
¼ head lettuce, torn into bite-size pieces
    (about 3 cups)
¼ cup toasted slivered almonds

HONEY DRESSING

¼ cup vegetable oil
2 tablespoons vinegar
1 tablespoon honey
¾ teaspoon salt
Dash of pepper
4 to 6 drops red pepper sauce

Prepare Honey Dressing. Toss with chicken, grapes, onions, green pepper and water chestnuts. Cover and refrigerate until chilled, at least 2 hours.

Toss chicken mixture with orange sections and lettuce. Spoon onto salad greens, if desired; sprinkle with almonds.

Shake all ingredients in tightly covered container.

Chicken-Orange-Avocado Salad

4 SERVINGS

1 small bunch romaine, torn into
    bite-size pieces (about 6 cups)
1½ cups cut-up cooked chicken
4 green onions (with tops), sliced (about
    ½ cup)
¼ cup sliced pimiento-stuffed olives
2 medium oranges or 1 medium
    grapefruit, pared and sectioned
½ cup mayonnaise or salad dressing
2 tablespoons orange juice
1 medium avocado
2 medium tomatoes, cut into wedges
Salt to taste

Place romaine, chicken, onions, olives and orange sections in large bowl; cover and refrigerate. Mix mayonnaise and orange juice; cover and refrigerate.

Just before serving, cut avocado into bite-size pieces. Toss avocado and tomato wedges with chicken mixture. Sprinkle with salt. Serve with mayonnaise mixture.

Following pages: Chicken-Orange-Avocado Salad

Oriental Chicken Salad

2 ounces uncooked maifun (rice stick)
  noodles*
Ginger Dressing (below)
1/2 bunch romaine, torn into bite-size
  pieces
2 cups cut-up cooked chicken
2 green onions (with tops), sliced (about
  1/4 cup)

GINGER DRESSING

1/4 cup vegetable oil
3 tablespoons vinegar
2 teaspoons sugar
1 teaspoon soy sauce
3/4 teaspoon salt
1/2 teaspoon pepper
1/4 teaspoon ground ginger

Prepare noodles as directed on package for deep-fried noodles; drain. Prepare Ginger Dressing; toss with noodles and the remaining ingredients.

*6 cups chow mein noodles can be substituted for the deep-fried maifun noodles; toss with Ginger Dressing and remaining ingredients.

Shake all ingredients in tightly covered container.

Hot Chicken Salad

2 cups cut-up cooked chicken
2 cups seasoned croutons
2 cups thinly sliced celery
1 cup mayonnaise or salad dressing
1/2 cup toasted slivered almonds
1 small onion, chopped (about 1/4 cup)
2 tablespoons lemon juice
1/2 teaspoon salt
1/2 cup shredded process American or
  Cheddar cheese (about 2 ounces)

Mix all ingredients except cheese in ungreased 2-quart casserole or rectangular baking dish, 12 × 7 1/2 × 2 inches. Sprinkle with cheese. Cook uncovered in 350° oven until hot, 30 to 35 minutes.

TO MICROWAVE: Mix all ingredients except cheese in 2-quart microwavable casserole. Sprinkle with cheese. Cover tightly and microwave on high (100%) 3 minutes; rotate casserole 1/2 turn. Microwave until hot, 4 to 6 minutes longer.

Chili-Chicken Salad

1 ½ cups cut-up cooked chicken
1 can (15 ½ ounces) kidney beans,
    drained
2 green onions (with tops), sliced (about
    ¼ cup)
1 small head iceberg lettuce or 10 ounces
    spinach, torn into bite-size pieces
Mexicali Dressing (below)
1 medium avocado
1 cup broken tortilla chips
1 medium tomato, cut into wedges
Pitted ripe olives

MEXICALI DRESSING

½ cup mayonnaise or salad dressing
¼ cup catsup
1 teaspoon chili powder
½ teaspoon garlic salt

Place chicken, beans, onions, and lettuce in large bowl. Cover and refrigerate at least 3 hours. Prepare Mexicali Dressing.

Just before serving, cut avocado into bite-size pieces. Toss avocado and dressing with chicken mixture. Sprinkle with tortilla chips; garnish with tomato wedges and olives.

CHEESY CHICKEN SALAD: Substitute ¾ cup shredded Cheddar or jalapeño pepper cheese (about 3 ounces) for ½ cup of the chicken.

Mix all ingredients; refrigerate.

· 6 ·

CHICKEN WITH PASTA

Chicken in Tarragon Cream

6 OR 7 SERVINGS

2½- to 3-pound broiler-fryer chicken, cut up
3 medium carrots, sliced (about 1½ cups)
1 cup Chicken Broth (page 8)
1 tablespoon snipped fresh tarragon or 1 teaspoon dried tarragon leaves
1½ teaspoons salt
⅛ teaspoon pepper
1 bay leaf
4 ounces mushrooms, sliced (about 1½ cups)
2 medium stalks celery, sliced (about 1 cup)
1 medium onion, sliced
½ cup dry white wine
½ cup half-and-half
3 tablespoons all-purpose flour
1 egg yolk
4 to 5 cups hot cooked noodles

Heat chicken, carrots, broth, tarragon, salt, pepper and bay leaf to boiling in 12-inch skillet or Dutch oven; reduce heat. Cover and simmer 30 minutes. Add mushrooms, celery and onion. Heat to boiling; reduce heat. Cover and simmer until thickest pieces of chicken are done, about 15 minutes.

Remove chicken and vegetables to warm platter with slotted spoon; keep warm. Drain liquid from skillet; strain and reserve 1 cup. Pour reserved liquid and the wine into skillet. Mix half-and-half, flour and egg yolk until smooth; stir into wine mixture. Cook over medium heat, stirring constantly, until thickened. Serve with chicken, vegetables and noodles.

Chicken Tetrazzini

¼ cup margarine or butter
¼ cup all-purpose flour
½ teaspoon salt
¼ teaspoon pepper
1 cup Chicken Broth (page 8)
1 cup whipping cream
2 tablespoons sherry
1 package (7 ounces) spaghetti, cooked
  and drained
2 cups cubed cooked chicken
1 jar (2.5 ounces) sliced mushrooms,
  drained
½ cup grated Parmesan cheese

Heat oven to 350°. Melt margarine in large saucepan over low heat. Blend in flour and seasonings. Cook over low heat, stirring until mixture is smooth and bubbly. Remove from heat. Stir in broth and cream. Heat to boiling, stirring constantly. Boil and stir 1 minute. Stir in wine, spaghetti, chicken and mushrooms.

Pour into ungreased 2-quart casserole. Sprinkle with cheese. Bake uncovered 30 minutes or until bubbly. To brown, place briefly under broiler.

Chicken-Pasta Primavera

1 cup chopped broccoli
⅓ cup chopped onion
2 cloves garlic, finely chopped
1 carrot, cut into very thin strips
3 tablespoons vegetable oil
2 cups cut-up cooked chicken
1 teaspoon salt
2 medium tomatoes, chopped
4 cups hot cooked macaroni shells or
  wheels
⅓ cup freshly grated Parmesan cheese
2 tablespoons snipped parsley

Cook and stir broccoli, onion, garlic and carrot in oil in 10-inch skillet over medium heat until broccoli is crisp-tender, about 10 minutes. Stir in chicken, salt and tomatoes; heat just until chicken is hot, about 3 minutes. Spoon chicken mixture over macaroni; sprinkle with cheese and parsley.

Following pages: Chicken-Pasta Primavera

Chicken-Cheese Lasagne

½ cup margarine or butter
2 cloves garlic, crushed
½ cup all-purpose flour
1 teaspoon salt
2 cups milk
2 cups Chicken Broth (page 8)
2 cups shredded mozzarella cheese (about
   8 ounces)
½ cup grated Parmesan cheese
1 medium onion, chopped (about ½ cup)
1 teaspoon dried basil leaves
½ teaspoon dried oregano leaves
¼ teaspoon pepper
8 ounces uncooked lasagne noodles (9 or
   10 noodles)
2 cups creamed cottage cheese (16
   ounces)
2 cups cut-up cooked chicken
2 packages (10 ounces each) frozen
   chopped spinach, thawed and well
   drained
½ cup grated Parmesan cheese

Heat margarine in 2-quart saucepan over low heat until melted; add garlic. Stir in flour and salt. Cook, stirring constantly, until bubbly. Remove from heat; stir in milk and broth. Heat to boiling, stirring constantly. Boil and stir 1 minute. Stir in mozzarella cheese, ½ cup Parmesan cheese, the onion, basil, oregano and pepper. Cook over low heat, stirring constantly, until mozzarella cheese is melted.

Spread ¼ of the cheese sauce (about 1½ cups) in ungreased rectangular baking dish, 13 × 9 × 2 inches; top with 3 or 4 uncooked noodles, overlapping if necessary. Spread half of the cottage cheese over noodles. Repeat with ¼ of the cheese sauce, 3 or 4 noodles and remaining cottage cheese. Top with chicken, spinach, ¼ of the cheese sauce, the remaining noodles and the remaining cheese sauce. Sprinkle with ½ cup Parmesan cheese. Cook uncovered in 350° oven until noodles are done, 35 to 40 minutes. Let stand 15 minutes before cutting.

Leek and Chicken Casserole

5 medium leeks or 2 medium onions,
  sliced
2 tablespoons margarine or butter
2 tablespoons all-purpose flour
1/2 teaspoon salt
1/4 teaspoon ground nutmeg
1/8 teaspoon pepper
1 cup Chicken Broth (page 8)
1 cup milk
3 cups cut-up cooked chicken
1/2 cup finely chopped fully cooked
  smoked ham
1 jar (2 ounces) diced pimiento, drained
3 cups hot cooked noodles
1 cup shredded Swiss cheese (about 4
  ounces)

Cook and stir leeks in margarine in 3-quart saucepan over medium heat until tender, about 5 minutes. Blend in flour, salt, nutmeg and pepper. Cook over low heat, stirring constantly, until bubbly; remove from heat. Stir in chicken broth and milk. Heat to boiling, stirring constantly. Boil and stir 1 minute. Stir in chicken, ham and pimiento. Spread about half of the chicken mixture in ungreased square pan, 9 × 9 × 2 inches, or 2½-quart casserole. Spoon noodles over chicken mixture; top with remaining chicken mixture. Sprinkle with cheese. Cook uncovered in 350° oven until cheese is light brown, 25 to 30 minutes.

Macaroni Casserole

1½ cups cut-up cooked chicken
1 cup shredded Cheddar cheese (4
  ounces)
1 cup milk
1/2 teaspoon salt
1/2 teaspoon curry powder
1 can (10¾ ounces) condensed cream of
  chicken soup
1 package (7 ounces) elbow macaroni
1 can (4 ounces) mushroom stems and
  pieces, undrained
1 jar (2 ounces) diced pimientos

Mix all ingredients in ungreased 1½-quart casserole or rectangular baking dish, 10 × 6 × 1½ inches. Cover and bake in 350° oven until macaroni is tender, 55 to 60 minutes.

TO MICROWAVE: Mix all ingredients in 3-quart microwavable casserole. Cover tightly and microwave on high (100%), stirring every 6 minutes, until macaroni is tender, 15 to 18 minutes. Let stand covered 5 minutes.

· 7 ·

SIMPLE SOUPS
AND SANDWICHES

Oriental-style Chicken Soup

4 SERVINGS (ABOUT 1¼ CUPS EACH)

*1 large whole chicken breast (about 1
  pound), skinned*
4½ cups water
1 tablespoon instant chicken bouillon
2 teaspoons soy sauce
¼ to ½ teaspoon ground ginger
½ teaspoon salt
1 medium carrot
1 cup sliced mushrooms (about 3 ounces)
*4 ounces Chinese pea pods, cut into
  1-inch pieces and tips removed (about
  1 cup)*
*3 green onions (with tops), cut into
  1½-inch pieces (about ½ cup)*
*2 ounces vermicelli, broken into 2-inch
  pieces (about ½ cup)**
*1 medium tomato, chopped (about ¾
  cup)*
1 cup shredded spinach, if desired

Heat chicken, water, bouillon (dry), soy sauce, ginger and salt to boiling in 3-quart saucepan; reduce heat. Cover and simmer until chicken is done, about 20 minutes.

Remove chicken from broth; cool chicken 10 minutes. Remove chicken from bones; cut chicken into pieces. Skim fat from broth; strain broth, if desired. Cut carrot lengthwise into ¼-inch strips, then crosswise into 1½-inch pieces.

Heat broth, carrot, mushrooms, pea pods, onions and vermicelli to boiling; reduce heat. Cover and simmer until vermicelli is done and vegetables are crisp-tender, 4 to 6 minutes. Add chicken, tomato and spinach; heat thoroughly.

*Vermicelli is a very thin spaghetti. Two ounces regular spaghetti, broken into 2-inch pieces, or ⅓ cup shell or ring macaroni can be substituted for the vermicelli; increase cooking time as directed on package. For crisp-tender vegetables, add during last 4 to 6 minutes of cooking time.

Chicken-Vegetable Chowder

1 package (10 ounces) frozen chopped
  broccoli
3 medium stalks celery, thinly sliced
  (about 2 cups)
1 medium onion, chopped (about 1/2 cup)
2 cups water
1 teaspoon salt
1 can (10 3/4 ounces) condensed chicken
  broth or 1 1/4 cups Chicken Broth
  (page 8)
1 cup cold milk
1/2 cup all-purpose flour
1 1/2 cups cut-up cooked chicken
1 cup milk
6 ounces Swiss cheese, cut into cubes
  (about 1 1/2 cups)

Rinse broccoli under running cold water to separate; drain. Heat broccoli, celery, onion, water, salt and broth to boiling in Dutch oven; reduce heat. Cover and simmer 10 minutes.

Shake 1 cup cold milk and the flour in tightly covered container; gradually stir into hot mixture. Heat to boiling. Boil and stir 1 minute. Stir in chicken and 1 cup milk. Heat over low heat, stirring occasionally, just until hot, about 10 minutes. Stir in cheese; let stand just until cheese is melted, 3 to 5 minutes; stir.

Brunswick-style Stew

1 pound bulk pork sausage
6 chicken legs (about 3 pounds)
1 cup water
1 large onion, sliced
2 medium stalks celery, sliced (about 1
  cup)
1 bay leaf
1 teaspoon dried basil leaves
1/2 teaspoon salt
1/2 teaspoon red pepper sauce
1 can (16 ounces) whole tomatoes
1 package (10 ounces) frozen whole
  kernel corn
1 package (10 ounces) frozen baby lima
  beans
2 tablespoons snipped parsley

Cook and stir sausage in 4-quart Dutch oven until brown. Remove with slotted spoon; reserve. Pour off all but 1 tablespoon fat. Cook legs in fat, turning occasionally, until golden brown. Add water, onion, celery, bay leaf, basil, salt, pepper sauce and reserved sausage. Heat to boiling; reduce heat. Cover and simmer until chicken is tender, 45 minutes. Remove chicken; cool slightly. Remove meat from skin and bones; cut meat into bite-size pieces. Return meat to Dutch oven; add tomatoes (with liquid), corn and lima beans. Break tomatoes up with fork. Heat to boiling; reduce heat. Cover and simmer until vegetables are tender, about 10 minutes. Sprinkle with parsley.

Following pages: Brunswick-style Stew

Mulligatawny Soup

2 1/2- to 3-pound broiler-fryer chicken,
  cut up
4 cups water
1 1/2 teaspoons salt
1 teaspoon curry powder
1 teaspoon lemon juice
1/8 teaspoon ground cloves
1/8 teaspoon ground mace
1 medium onion, chopped (about 1/2 cup)
2 tablespoons margarine or butter
2 tablespoons all-purpose flour
2 medium tomatoes, chopped
1 medium carrot, thinly sliced
1 medium apple, chopped
1 medium green pepper, cut into 1/2-inch
  pieces
Snipped parsley

Remove any excess fat from chicken. Heat chicken, water, salt, curry powder, lemon juice, cloves and mace to boiling in Dutch oven; reduce heat. Cover and simmer until thickest pieces of chicken are done, about 45 minutes. Remove chicken from broth; cool chicken 10 minutes. Skim fat from broth. Add enough water to broth, if necessary, to measure 4 cups. Remove chicken from bones and skin; cut chicken into pieces.

Cook and stir onion in margarine in another Dutch oven until tender. Remove from heat; stir in flour. Gradually stir in broth. Add chicken, tomatoes, carrot, apple and green pepper. Heat to boiling; reduce heat. Cover and simmer until carrot is tender, about 10 minutes. Garnish with parsley.

Chicken and Vegetable Soup

6 cups Chicken Broth (page 8)
2 cups cut-up cooked chicken
1/2 teaspoon salt
1/2 teaspoon garlic salt
1/2 teaspoon dried basil leaves
1/4 teaspoon pepper
3 medium carrots, cut into 3 × 1/4-inch
  strips
3 small onions, sliced
1 package (10 ounces) frozen cut green
  beans
1/2 cup uncooked small macaroni rings
4 small zucchini, cut into 1/4-inch slices

Heat all ingredients except macaroni and zucchini to boiling in Dutch oven; reduce heat. Cover and simmer 20 minutes. Stir in macaroni and zucchini. Heat to boiling; reduce heat. Cover and simmer until macaroni is tender, about 10 minutes.

Chicken Pocket Sandwiches

6 SERVINGS

1/2 cup plain yogurt
1 tablespoon snipped chives or chopped
  onion
1 tablespoon lemon juice
1 teaspoon garlic salt
3 drops red pepper sauce
1 1/2 cups cut-up cooked chicken
1 cup shredded natural Swiss, Monterey
  Jack or Cheddar cheese (about 4
  ounces)
1 medium avocado, cut up
1 medium tomato, coarsely chopped
6 pocket breads
1 cup alfalfa sprouts or shredded lettuce

Mix yogurt, chives, lemon juice, garlic salt and pepper sauce; toss with chicken, cheese, avocado and tomato. Cut or tear pocket breads into halves. Alternate chicken mixture and alfalfa sprouts in pocket bread halves, allowing about 1/4 cup chicken mixture in each half.

Chicken Reuben Sandwiches

4 SANDWICHES

1/4 cup Thousand Island dressing
8 slices rye or pumpernickel bread
4 slices natural Swiss cheese
4 slices cooked chicken
1 cup sauerkraut, drained

Spread dressing over 4 slices bread; top with cheese, chicken and sauerkraut. Top with remaining slices bread. (If desired, spread margarine or butter over both sides of each sandwich.) Cook uncovered in skillet over low heat until bottoms are golden brown and cheese begins to melt, 5 to 7 minutes on each side.

CHICKEN RACHEL SANDWICHES: Substitute 1 cup coleslaw for the sauerkraut.

Following pages: Chicken Pocket Sandwich

Chicken Barbecue Sandwiches

1/2 cup catsup
1/4 cup vinegar
2 tablespoons chopped onion
1 tablespoon Worcestershire sauce
1 teaspoon packed brown sugar
1/4 teaspoon dry mustard
1 clove garlic, crushed
1 1/2 cups cut-up cooked chicken*
4 hamburger buns, split

Heat all ingredients except chicken and buns to boiling over medium heat, stirring constantly; reduce heat. Simmer uncovered, stirring occasionally, 10 minutes; stir in chicken. Cover and simmer until chicken is hot, about 5 minutes. Fill hamburger buns with chicken mixture.

*3 packages (3 ounces each) thinly sliced smoked chicken, cut into 1-inch strips, can be substituted for the 1 1/2 cups cut-up chicken.

Chicken Tostadas

6 six-inch tostada shells
1 can (16 ounces) refried beans
1 1/2 cups cut-up cooked chicken
1 teaspoon chili powder
1/2 teaspoon dried oregano leaves
1/2 teaspoon salt
1/4 teaspoon ground cumin
1 can (8 ounces) tomato sauce
1 medium avocado
Lemon juice
3/4 cup shredded Cheddar or Monterey
   Jack cheese (about 3 ounces)
2 medium tomatoes, sliced
3 cups shredded lettuce
Dairy sour cream
Hot taco sauce

Heat tostada shells as directed on package. Heat beans over medium heat until hot. Heat chicken, chili powder, oregano leaves, salt, cumin and tomato sauce until hot. Cut avocado lengthwise into slices; sprinkle with lemon juice.

Spread about 1/4 cup of the beans on each tostada shell; spread with about 1/4 cup chicken mixture. Sprinkle 2 tablespoons cheese over each. Arrange tomato and avocado slices and lettuce on top. Serve with sour cream and taco sauce.

Note: If desired, tostadas can be broiled after sprinkling with cheese. Set oven control to broil and/or 550°. Broil tostadas with tops 2 to 3 inches from heat just until cheese is melted, 1 to 2 minutes. Top with tomato and avocado slices and shredded lettuce.

RED SPOON TIPS

Plump, juicy chicken is a comforting food. Surprisingly, it is as versatile as it is economical. Chicken is glorious when fancied up and luscious when simple. Chicken calls for nothing in the way of elaborate preparation, and gives delicious, satisfying results time after time.

More than many foods, chicken demands careful handling and consideration when it comes to food safety measures. Chicken is hospitable to the bacteria that cause food poisoning, so it is important to take precautions against spoiling. Fresh chicken is perishable. Store it in the coldest spot in the refrigerator for no longer than 2 days after purchasing it. When buying chicken to keep on hand for later use, freeze it.

Cooked chicken is perishable, too, especially in dishes containing eggs, milk or salad dressing. The United States Department of Agriculture recommends that hot foods should be kept hot (above 140 degrees) and cold foods cold (below 40 degrees). Don't keep any food, whether hot or cold, at room temperature for longer than 2 hours; bacteria thrive in lukewarm food.

To cool hot chicken dishes, don't let them sit at room temperature. Instead, small- or medium-size quantities can be re-frigerated immediately. Large quantities of hot food (which may raise refrigerator temperatures to unacceptable levels) may be cooled by placing the food in a container that is set into a large bowl or sink of cold water and ice.

The bacteria in raw chicken can be transmitted to other foods via kitchen utensils. To prevent the transfer of bacteria use a nonporous plastic cutting board when slicing raw poultry and meat. Also, wash your hands with soap after handling raw chicken; this is especially critical if you go on to prepare foods that are not cooked (salad, for example). Thoroughly clean the cutting board, counter or kitchen surface and any utensils used in preparing chicken. Wash wooden cutting boards with a solution of 1 teaspoon chlorine bleach and ½ teaspoon vinegar to 2 quarts of water.

Storing Chicken

Raw chicken: Tray-packed chicken should be stored in its original wrapping in the refrigerator. Chicken wrapped in meat-market paper should be rinsed with cold water, patted dry and repackaged in plastic bags, plastic wrap or food storage containers. Refrigerate for no longer than 2 days.

Cooked chicken: Cover or wrap cooked chicken tightly and refrigerate it for no longer than 2 days. Chicken, giblets, stuffing and gravy should be stored in separate containers.

Freezing Chicken

Wrap raw or uncooked chicken tightly (not giblets—freeze them separately) in moisture-vapor-resistant freezer wrap, such as plastic freezer bags, freezer paper or heavy-duty aluminum foil. Press as much air as possible out of the package before sealing it. Mark the package with the date and then freeze.

Spoon casseroles or chicken in gravy or sauce into freezer containers with tight-fitting lids. (Casserole dishes that can be placed in the oven directly from the freezer are very handy.)

Cut-up cooked chicken should be frozen in broth to cover it, if it is to be stored for a month or longer. Do not stuff a chicken and freeze it for later roasting—always stuff chicken just before it is to be cooked.

Maximum Storage Times at 0° F

CHICKEN	STORAGE TIME
Cooked	
Creamed or in broth	3 to 4 months
No sauce or broth	1 month

Uncooked	
Cut up	4 to 6 months
Giblets	1 to 3 months
Whole	6 to 8 months
Broth	2 to 3 months

Menus for All Seasons

SPRING PICNIC

- Maryland Fried Chicken (page 14)
- Potato salad with celery seed
- Crudités: summer squash coins and tiny radishes
- Corn bread
- Seedless green grapes
- Brownies

AUTUMN PICNIC

- Country Broiled Chicken (page 40)
- Salad of Harvard beets
- Deviled eggs
- Whole grain rolls
- Crisp greening apples with Cheddar cheese
- Ginger snap cookies

DINNER AT EIGHT

- Chicken and Artichoke Fondue (page 59)
- Fluffy white rice
- Acorn squash purée
- Salad of romaine and mushrooms
- Parker house rolls
- Chocolate mousse with raspberry sauce

Sunday Supper

- Chicken Fricassee with Chive Dumplings (page 26)
- Homemade mashed potatoes
- Fresh peas
- Date-nut bread
- Pear salad with blue cheese crumbles
- Angel food cake with crushed strawberries

South of the Border

- Chicken Chili (page 36)
- Soft flour tortillas
- Avocado, red onion and orange salad
- Fresh fruit sherbet

A La Mode

- Coq au Vin (page 18)
- New potatoes with parsley
- Steamed fresh asparagus
- French baguettes
- Mixed greens with mustard vinaigrette
- Apple tart

Turkey Talk

Turkey may be substituted for chicken in all of the following recipes.

- Chicken à la King
- Chicken Chili
- Chicken Curry
- Chicken and Corn Casserole
- Chicken and Wild Rice Casserole
- Chicken with Phyllo
- Chicken Enchiladas
- Chicken-Sausage Pies
- Leek and Chicken Casserole
- Classic Chicken Divan
- Mexican Chicken in Crust
- Chicken in Potato Shells
- Spinach and Chicken Casserole
- Chili-Chicken Salad
- Club Salad
- Hot Chicken Salad
- Oriental Chicken Salad
- Chicken-Orange-Avocado Salad
- Chicken Salad with Honey Dressing
- Chicken-Cheese Lasagne
- Chicken Tetrazzini
- Chicken-Pasta Primavera
- Macaroni Casserole
- Pasta with Pesto Chicken
- Chicken and Vegetable Soup
- Chicken-Vegetable Chowder
- Chicken Tostadas
- Creamy Chicken-filled Croissants
- Chicken Reuben Sandwiches
- Chicken Pocket Sandwiches

Cutting a Whole Chicken into Parts

Cutting up a chicken at home is less expensive than buying a chicken cut into parts. It is easy, too. The one essential tool for the job is a sharp utility knife of medium size. Special boning knives (designed with particularly narrow blades) are helpful, but not absolutely necessary. Don't try to cut a frozen chicken into parts; it is too difficult to control the knife.

Place the whole chicken, breast up, on a clean, dry cutting board. Trim away fat as you cut up the chicken. If the recipe doesn't call for browning the chicken pieces or if you are making a soup or stew, you may wish to remove the skin.

Now that you have cleaned the chicken, we will take you through cutting a chicken into its various parts.

1. To remove the wings, cut into the joint, rolling the knife so that the blade follows the curve of the joint (fig. 1).

2. To remove the legs, position the knife between the thigh and the body of the chicken. Cut through the skin and continue cutting through the meat between the tail and the hip joint, cutting as close to the backbone as possible. Bend the leg back until the hip joint pops out (fig. 2).

3. Continue cutting around the bone, pulling the leg from the body until the meat is separated from the bone (fig. 3). Cut through the remaining skin and free the leg.

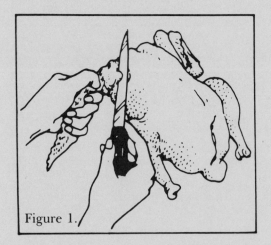

Figure 1.

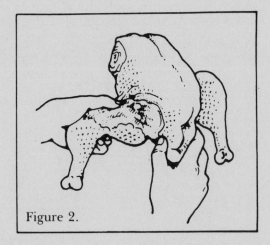

Figure 2.

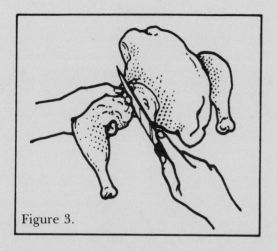

Figure 3.

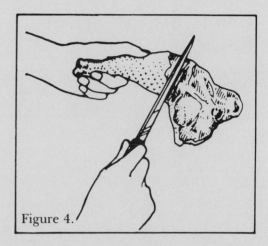

Figure 4.

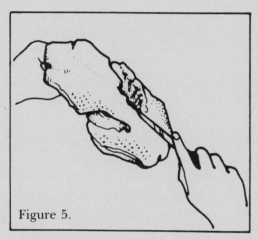

Figure 5.

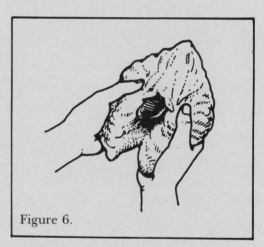

Figure 6.

4. To separate the thighs from the drumsticks, make a cut about ⅛ inch from the fat line toward the drumstick (fig. 4). (Look for a thin, whitish line that runs across the joint.)

5. To separate the back from the breast, hold the body neck-end down and cut downward along each side of the backbone through the rib joints (fig. 5).

6. Place the breast skin-side down and cut just through the white cartilage at the V of the neck. Bend the breast halves back until the keel bone (the dark bone at the center of the breast) pops away from the meat. Remove the keel bone (for more detail see step 2, page 102). Cut the breast into halves through the wishbone; use kitchen scissors for this, if preferred (fig. 6).

How to Bone a Chicken Breast

Chicken breasts can be purchased whole or split into halves. If starting with a split breast, follow the instructions for boning beginning with step 3. Otherwise, use a sharp knife with a thin blade, ideally no longer than 6 inches, and do the following:

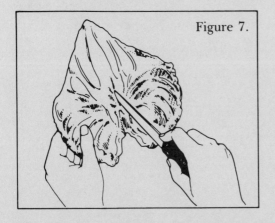

Figure 7.

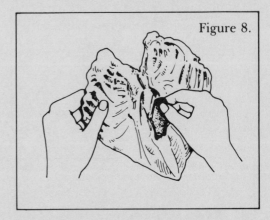

Figure 8.

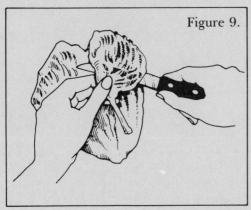

Figure 9.

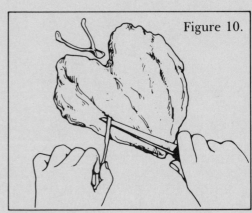

Figure 10.

1. Place a whole chicken breast, skin-side down, on a clean, dry cutting board. Cut just through the white cartilage at the **V** of the neck to expose the end of the keel bone (the dark bone at the center of the breast) (fig. 7).

2. Bend the breast halves back until the keel bone pops away from the meat. Run a finger along each side of the keel bone to loosen it. Pull the bone out; if it comes out in pieces, that is fine (fig. 8).

3. To remove the rib cages, insert the point of the knife under the long rib bone. Cut the rib cage away from the meat. Cut through the shoulder joint to free the entire rib cage (fig. 9).

4. Turn the chicken breast over and remove the skin. Cut away the wishbone. Slip the knife under the white tendons on either side of the breast; loosen and pull out the tendons. Cut the breast into halves (fig. 10).

How to Truss a Chicken

Why truss a chicken in the first place? It makes for a more elegant bird. An untrussed chicken will have its wings and legs drooping at odd angles when roasted. If the bird is stuffed, trussing it can help keep the stuffing where it belongs—inside the body cavity. However, if you prefer not to truss chicken, test for doneness somewhat sooner. Tying the legs up against the bird's body results in a longer roasting time.

If stuffing the chicken, fill the wishbone area first. With a metal skewer, fasten the neck skin to the back of the chicken. Lift the wings up and fold them over the back so that the tips are touching. Fill the body cavity lightly with stuffing, if desired. Skewer the drumsticks to the tail, or tie the drumsticks together with a length of kitchen string.

Timetable For Roasting

READY-TO-COOK WEIGHT	OVEN TEMPERATURE	APPROXIMATE TIME
BROILER-FRYER		
1½ to 2 pounds	400°F	¾ to 1 hour
2 to 2½ pounds	400°F	1 to 1¼ hours
2½ to 3 pounds	375°F	1¼ to 1¾ hours
3 to 4 pounds	375°F	1¾ to 2¼ hours
CAPON (STUFFED)		
5 to 8 pounds	325°F	2½ to 3½ hours
DUCK		
3½ pounds	350°F	2 hours
5½ pounds	350°F	3 hours
GOOSE		
7 to 9 pounds	350°F	2½ to 3 hours
9 to 11 pounds	350°F	3 to 3½ hours
11 to 13 pounds	350°F	3½ to 4 hours

Note: Times given are for unstuffed chickens, ducks or geese; stuffed birds require 15 to 30 minutes longer.

Carving

How often it is referred to as "the art of carving"! Knowing how to carve is a handy skill, and being able to do it with grace at the table is an accomplishment. Carving does, however, have the reputation for being difficult or somehow unpredictable, and nothing could be further from the truth.

If carving in the kitchen, place the roast chicken (or turkey, duck or pheasant) breast up, on a clean, dry cutting board. This is a bit easier than carving the bird on the serving platter, as there is more room to maneuver. If carving at the table, make sure that the serving platter sits on a mat or trivet that won't slip suddenly under the movement of the knife.

The tools needed for carving are few, but important: a very sharp carving knife, and a fork with long prongs. Special carving forks have a knife-guard that flips up from the handle, protecting the hand if the knife should slip.

Place the chicken, breast up, with the legs pointing toward the carver's right if the carver is right-handed (if left-handed, turn the chicken so that the legs point toward the carver's left). Remove any kitchen string or skewers.

Gently pull one leg away from the body while cutting through the joint between the leg and the body. Remove the leg. Separate the drumstick from the thigh by cutting through that joint.

Make a deep horizontal cut (parallel to the table surface) into the breast just above the wing on the same side. Insert the fork into the top of the breast to hold the chicken steady (as shown). Starting halfway up the breast, carve thin slices down to the horizontal cut. Repeat on the other side.

All-Time Favorite Chicken Recipes

COMPANY FARE

- French Chicken Fricassee
- Chicken Piccata
- Lemon Chicken
- Chicken with Golden Pilaf
- Chicken Curry
- Chicken with Artichokes and Grapes
- Chicken with Asparagus Béarnaise
- Oven-fried Chicken with Herb Biscuits
- Chicken with Apricots
- Chicken Rolls with Pork Stuffing
- Chicken and Artichoke Fondue

FAMILY FAVORITES

- Batter-fried Chicken
- Golden Chicken Nuggets
- Chicken à la King
- Chicken Fricassee with Chive Dumplings
- Chicken Paprika
- Country Broiled Chicken
- Glazed Chicken Drumsticks
- Chicken in Potato Shells
- Chicken and Corn Casserole
- Classic Chicken Divan
- Chicken-Sausage Pies
- Herbed Lemon Chicken
- Chicken with Gravy
- Savory Rock Cornish Hens
- Macaroni Casserole
- Chicken Barbecue Sandwiches

PERFECT FOR "COVERED DISH" OR POTLUCK SUPPERS

- Fried Chicken
- Chicken Ratatouille
- Chicken and Peppers
- Jambalaya
- Mexican-style Chicken
- Chicken Chili
- Oven-barbecued Chicken
- Mexican Chicken in Crust
- Chicken and Rice with Curry Sauce
- Chicken Tetrazzini
- Leek and Chicken Casserole

INTERNATIONAL FLAIR

- Stir-fried Chicken and Vegetables
- Coq au Vin
- Chicken Cacciatore
- Chicken Ratatouille
- Chicken Provençal
- French Chicken Fricassee
- Chicken Piccata
- Chicken Almond
- Paella
- Mexican-style Chicken
- Chicken Curry
- Couscous
- Cornmeal Chicken
- Tandoori-style Chicken
- Sweet and Sour Chicken
- Chicken Teriyaki
- Arroz con Pollo
- Chicken Enchiladas
- Oriental-style Chicken Soup

Giblets

Most people have heard of giblets; many have eaten them with relish. Few could tell you what a giblet *is*. Giblets, collectively, are the liver, heart and gizzard of a chicken. Strictly speaking, the term *giblets* includes the pinions, or wing tips, too; for some reason, people rarely bother to remove wing tips any longer, although they certainly add flavor. The gizzard is part of the bird's digestive tract—the third pouch, to be exact.

Giblets may be stored frozen. As with any chicken parts, let them thaw in the refrigerator rather than at room temperature. To store chicken livers in quantity, freeze them covered with milk.

Chicken Livers and Rice

4 TO 6 SERVINGS

3 small onions, chopped (about ¾ cup)
1 medium stalk celery, chopped (about ½ cup)
1 can (4 ounces) mushroom stems and pieces, drained, or 4 ounces fresh mushrooms, sliced
2 tablespoons margarine or butter
2 cans (10¾ ounces each) condensed chicken broth
1 package (6 ounces) long-grain and wild rice mix (with seasoning)
4 slices bacon
1 pound chicken livers
¼ cup all-purpose flour

Cook and stir onions, celery and mushrooms in margarine in 2-quart saucepan until onions are tender; stir in chicken broth. Heat to boiling. Place rice and seasoning mix in ungreased 2-quart casserole or rectangular baking dish, 12 × 7½ × 2 inches. Stir broth mixture into rice. Cover and cook in 350° oven 30 minutes.

Fry bacon until crisp; drain and crumble. Coat livers with flour; cook and stir in bacon fat until brown. Arrange livers on rice around edge of casserole. Cover and cook until rice is tender and liquid is absorbed, about 25 minutes. Sprinkle with bacon.

Chicken Gizzards with Vegetables

1 pound chicken gizzards
1½ cups water
¼ teaspoon salt
¼ cup all-purpose flour
¼ teaspoon garlic powder
¼ teaspoon pepper
2 tablespoons margarine, butter or vegetable oil
2 medium carrots, thinly sliced (about 1 cup)
2 medium stalks celery, sliced (about 1 cup)
1 small onion, sliced
2 tablespoons soy sauce
1 tablespoon lemon juice
2 teaspoons cornstarch
2 tablespoons chopped pimientos, if desired

Heat gizzards, water and salt to boiling; reduce heat. Cover and simmer until gizzards are fork-tender, 1 to 1½ hours. Remove gizzards from broth; reserve broth. Cool gizzards 10 minutes; cut into bite-size pieces, discarding any gristle. Pat gizzards dry. Mix flour, garlic powder and pepper; coat gizzards.

Heat margarine in 10-inch skillet over medium heat until melted. Cook and stir gizzards in margarine until golden brown, about 10 minutes. Remove gizzards from skillet; keep warm. Add enough water to broth, if necessary, to measure 1 cup. Add broth, carrots, celery and onion to skillet. Heat to boiling; reduce heat. Cover and simmer 5 minutes. Mix soy sauce, lemon juice and cornstarch; stir into skillet. Heat to boiling, stirring constantly. Boil and stir 1 minute. Stir in gizzards and pimientos. Serve with hot cooked rice, if desired.

Nutritional Value of Chicken

The Recommended Dietary Allowance (RDA) for protein is 65 grams a day. The chart below indicates the nutritive breakdown of chicken by parts.

Relatively low-calorie chicken can be made even more so when excess fat is trimmed and the skin is removed. On average, removing the skin from 3 ounces of chicken reduces calories by 70. For example, a 3-ounce portion of broiled chicken breast has 185 calories; removing the skin reduces the calorie count to 115.

Chicken Parts (including bone)	Protein (grams)	Fat (grams)	Calories	Carbohydrate (grams)
Half breast (6 ounces)	27.6	3.23	147.7	———
Drumstick (4 ounces)	12.8	2.65	78.2	———
Thigh (4 ounces)	15.4	4.77	108.7	———
Wing	5.13	2.06	40.6	———

INDEX

Credits

V.P., Associate Publisher: Anne M. Zeman
Project Editor: Rebecca W. Atwater
Creative Director: J.C. Suarès
Photographer: Anthony Johnson
Designer: Patricia Fabricant
Production Editor: Kimberly Ebert

112

WORTH
20
COUPON
POINTS

For Betty
Crocker Catalog,
send 50¢ (no
stamps) with your
name and address to:
General Mills, Box 59078,
Minneapolis, MN 55459.
Redeemable with cash by U.S.
purchaser of product before April,
1999. Void where prohibited, taxed
or regulated. **S**

BETTY CROCKER COUPON